To

TINA

All the best.

YES, WE'RE OPEN

DEFENDING THE SMALL BUSINESS
UNDER SIEGE

William M[/]

9/6/03

Who should read *Yes, We're Open?*

Yes, We're Open is a must for anyone struggling to keep a small business alive. It will also be very valuable to anyone who owns a small business, is thinking about starting a new business, or has been asked to invest in one.

Is your small business in trouble?

Yes, We're Open provides practical advice on what to do when you realizes your small business is in trouble. Don't give up! You may still be able to turn your business around and make it thrive.

Thinking about starting a business?

Setting up a new business correctly is important to its ultimate success. *Yes, We're Open* will provide you with dozens of examples of how small businesses have been poorly set up and the consequences they suffered as a result. It will also suggest ways to start your business on a sound footing and operate it effectively.

Want to better understand the small business owner?

In *Yes, We're Open*, Attorney William Manchee shares his insights acquired over the past twenty-five years representing hundreds of small business owners in a myriad of situations. Learn valuable lessons through dozens of stories inspired by actual cases from the past.

To my sister

Darline Morris-Baldwin

who has been a staunch supporter
from the first day I logged on
the computer and began my
writing career.

YES, WE'RE OPEN

DEFENDING THE SMALL BUSINESS
UNDER SIEGE

By
William Manchee, J.D.

Edited by
Mary Klaasen, Ph.D.

Top Publications, Ltd.
Dallas, Texas

Yes, We're Open

A Top Publications Paperback

First Edition

Top Publications, Ltd.
12221 Merit Drive, Suite 750
Dallas, Texas 75251

ISBN 1-929976-24-0

Library of Congress Control Number 2003105215

Printed in the United States of America

CONTENTS

Poems

Be Free

America, land of the free.
But is that true for you and me?
Got to work to survive
In by nine, out by five

Can't be late, punch the clock
Work all day, shelves to stock
Shuffle paper here and there
Fold it, file it, mail it everywhere

Do this, do that. What'd you say?
Overtime? We have to stay?
Work, work, work, day and night
Got bills to pay, oh that's right

Tired of working, hate our plight?
Lets start a business, yes, that's right
Be independent, on our own
Not a greedy corporate drone

Come and go as we wish
Take a hike, catch some fish
No one cares, we're the boss
Lose a buck? That's our loss

Now we're free, free at last
Self-employed, what a blast
America, land of the free
At least that's so, for you and me

INTRODUCTION

Owning a successful small business is everyone's dream at one time or another. For only the business owner is truly free. If you work for someone else, your life and destiny are in their hands. With little, if any, notice they can lay you off, making years of hard work meaningless. Or they can promise you the stars and then pass you by like a beggar on the street. But if you work for yourself, you are truly free—free to carve your own destiny and to go as far as your talents and ambition will take you.

Over the years I have presided over the births and deaths of hundreds of small businesses. As an attorney, I have watched many of them grow, mature, and thrive, but I have seen many more stumble, fall, and die.

It is painful to see an entrepreneur, once so full of hope and excitement, suddenly desperate and defeated. I am saddened when I drive down the street and see an empty storefront, as I know someone has suffered an immeasurable loss, and endured extraordinary grief and pain trying to save their piece of the American dream.

There are few experiences in life as painful and brutal as the failure of a small business. For a small business conceived and nurtured by its owner is like a living, breathing child. Its loss is no less traumatic than losing a loved one. After all, a business owner spends most of his waking hours at work. He will invariably become very attached to it, particularly if it is the business he loves and the one he has always wanted to pursue.

Inevitably the business becomes an extension of the owner himself. When it is ailing, he is ailing as well from stress and worry over whatever problems the business is facing. When the business is thriving, he will be happy, confident, and enjoying life to the fullest. If the business fails, the owner will feel like a failure and suffer deep emotional scars that will greatly impact his personal life for years to come.

With business failure often comes marital strife and divorce. I don't claim to be a psychologist, but every day I see husbands and wives torn apart because one blames the other for a business failure. Or, if they don't blame each other, they are often so tired and battered from battling with creditors that they give up on the marriage. The sight of each other only brings back bad memories. So too often the unhappy couple opts for divorce. If the marriage does survive, it will never be the same.

Having watched my small business clients closely over the years and having operated my own law practice, I have come to some conclusions about why some businesses succeed while others fail. The sad fact is that many of the businesses I have seen fail could have been successful. The good news is that it's not too late for those still in business, if they will wake up and take control of their destiny.

Don't get me wrong. This book doesn't contain any magical formula for success. Turning a business around requires hard work, discipline, and sacrifice. But what I hope this book will do is give the reader insight into why so many small businesses fail, and provide solutions and strategies that can help turn around an ailing business.

This book is intentionally written in a simple, informal style for the average business owner rather than for college graduates or MBAs. I've found that the cause of business failure isn't just a lack of education, experience, or business training, but just as often a lack of common sense. Often small business owners, or "SBO"s as I will call them from now on, do things they know are stupid and reckless. Why? Because entrepreneurs by definition are risk-takers. They like to experiment and do brash things that may only have a slim chance of success. They are the eternal optimist and often have unrealistic expectations.

Obviously there are a lot of different kinds of small businesses, but for the purpose of this book that doesn't matter. I don't intend to dissect the workings of any particular type of business. I have found that most people who go into a business know the basics of that particular business. They have either worked for someone else in that field or have been trained somehow to perform their trade. What they usually are lacking is basic business training, education, or experience.

The knowledge I have learned over the years has come primarily from trial and error, rather than from a textbook. Sometimes I've learned from my own mistakes, but more often it has been from the mistakes of my clients. Unfortunately, my clients usually come to me after they are in trouble rather than consulting with me in the beginning, and possibly avoiding the problems that now confront them.

Although my major at UCLA back in the late 60s was political science, fortunately, I did minor in economics. The business courses I took were helpful to me when I started in law practice in 1976. More importantly, however, was the training I received at Metropolitan Life Insurance Company. While I was in law school I had to support my wife and four children, so I worked full time selling life insurance. This wasn't a glamorous job, but I did learn much about financial and business planning—something that had scarcely been mentioned in high school or college.

This book is not intended to be a manual or reference book. It is my hope that it will be interesting, entertaining, and informative. I fear too many self-help books get stuck on a shelf and never read cover-to-cover because they are too much like a textbook. This book is about adversity and how to overcome it. Its full of practical advice and ideas on how to deal with just about every adversity an SBO might face.

Yes, We're Open is full of real life events that should be of interest to any SBO. Obviously, the names and locations have been changed and the facts altered enough such that no confidences will be breached. Hopefully, you will be able to identify with the characters in these stories and understand the problems they face. If you are a SBO, you will no doubt be facing similar problems and can learn from the mistakes made by the SBOs in these stories.

As needed, I will provide legal and business advice but it will not be technical or hard to understand. It is not my intention to burden you with the complexities of the law, but simply to give you ideas and alternatives that will provide direction and avenues to take toward solving the problems faced by SBOs.

I consider every business failure a tragedy and, when it is one of my clients who goes down, it is even more troubling. I often lie awake at night wondering if there was something else I could have done to save a client's business and spare him and his family the dire consequences of a business failure. My only hope is that this book will help other SBOs save their small businesses so they can live truly free and remain in control of their destiny.

PART 1

WHY SMALL BUSINESSES FAIL

Chapter 1

Doomed from Day One

Many small businesses are doomed from day one—not from competition or the economy, but from their owners. From the moment they proudly frame their first dollar made and hang it on the wall, it is just a matter of time, days, weeks, or months before their business fails. When the doors open, they are full of excitement and hope, and expect only wonderful things to happen to them. Unfortunately, their destiny is already decided because they have no idea how a business should be operated.

I have a friend who is an amateur pilot. He loves flying and has a small plane that he meticulously maintains and flies on the weekends. He has logged hundreds of hours and I feel very comfortable flying with him. If anything were to go wrong, he would know what to do. I, on the other hand, know nothing about airplanes and if he were to have a heart attack while we were flying together, we would be in serious trouble. Sure I've watched him fly the plane and it looks pretty easy, but the reality is that flying a plane is a very complicated and tricky business. Odds are I would crash the plane and we would both perish.

Many businesses look deceptively simple and people think they will be easy to run. Rarely is that the case. Running a business without training and experience can be as tricky and dangerous as piloting an airplane for the very first time. Yet every day thousands of entrepreneurs embark on new business ventures with a vision but without a plan, with hope but without a realistic likelihood of success.

One of my old clients, Roger Blake, is a plumber. He and his wife, Jane, have been running their small plumbing business for years. They do primarily subcontract work for home builders and have a good reputation. Jane handles the day-to-day operation of the business and Roger oversees all the actual plumbing.

Several years ago there was a period of six or eight months in Dallas where new construction almost came to a standstill. During this stretch Roger and Jane got behind on their mortgage payments and lost their home. Jane was so upset about it, she left Roger to do some thinking about the future.

Roger was lost without Jane. Not only did he not know how to run a business, he didn't have time to do his and Jane's job too. Both Roger and Jane were necessary for the business to be successful. So I told Roger he had three choices: to reconcile with Jane, hire someone who could do what Jane had done for the business, or learn Jane's job and work 18 hours a day.

In today's world opportunities abound for learning how to run a small business. The libraries and bookstores are full of books on the subject. Colleges and private institutions provide classes and training on almost every aspect of operating a business. The small business administration and other government agencies also have books, periodicals and training on various aspects of running a business. These educational and training opportunities require a time commitment, however, that may not be feasible. This was the case with Roger.

Roger and Jane eventually reconciled. Unfortunately, by the time they got their business operating smoothly again, they were way behind on their bills and had little hope of catching up. To give them time to recover I suggested they file a chapter 13 debtor adjustment which is a form of personal bankruptcy in which you are allowed to continue to run a small business. Under chapter 13 they were able to keep their creditors at bay and pay out what they owed over five years.

During this time I suggested Roger learn everything that Jane did for the business in case for any reason she couldn't perform those functions in the future. It wasn't that I was pessimistic about his marriage, but I wanted him to appreciate the contribution she was making to the business and to take her more seriously. Then if she did leave him, he would be able do her job until he could hire someone to take her place or find a new partner.

Chapter 2

Looting

From my observation over the years, looting is the primary reason small businesses fail. Looting results from the mistaken belief that the SBO is owed a certain standard of living. Usually there hasn't been a study or budget projection done to determine what compensation the business can support. The owner either sets an arbitrary salary or takes money from the business as he needs it. Either way the business starts to slowly wither as the owner pockets precious operating capital until there isn't enough left to pay the bills as they come due.

Several years ago I represented a corporation that had been wholesaling gift items to retailers. There were four owners, all who were previously employed by a another very successful company in the same business. Over the years they came to realize that their hard work and skill was making their employer very rich. This realization caused them to ask for pay raises and better fringe benefits, which the owner refused to give them.

They were bitter and frustrated over this and, one day a few months later, they all decided they knew enough to quit and go into competition with their employer. Each of the four partners were well respected, knowledgeable in the trade, but none of them had ever operated a business before. Despite this handicap, their new enterprise flourished largely because they were able to take with them some very large customers.

Two years later when they came to see me, they were deeply in debt, owed substantial taxes to the IRS, and had been locked out by their landlord. As I was filling out a bankruptcy questionnaire, I asked them what compensation each was taking from the business. The CFO replied that each of the four stockholders had an annual salary of $150,000 and, of course, each was provided a Mercedes. When I quizzed them further I found there were only a half dozen other employees all earning less than $30,000 a year.

Common sense should have told them they didn't have a prayer of survival with this type of a cash flow drain, but each was used to a big salary with their previous employer and just assumed their new startup company could provide the same for them. What they should have done was not take a salary and split eighty percent of the profits each quarter. This might have been painful to them, but at least the business would have had a chance of survival.

This is an extreme example of looting. Usually it is less obvious. For example, one of my first clients was a fine tailor from Italy, Gino Ricardo. He was always very busy, often working ten or twelve hours a day. Operating as a sole proprietor, he had only one checking account from which he paid all his personal and business expenses. Being good Catholics, they had many children, and as their kids got older, household expenses rose dramatically. Soon the business started to have cash flow problems. The rent was late, tax deposits were missed, the electric company was threatening to cut off the power, and checks were bouncing. That's when Gino and his wife came to see me.

It was painful to see them in this situation as I had known them for several years. I met them while selling life insurance when I was in law school. I sold Gino my very first life insurance policy a week after I went to work for Metropolitan Life. Three years later when I hung up my shingle, they were there to have me draw up a will. They were very nice people and I loved all their kids.

The first thing I do when a client with financial problems comes to see me is create a budget. It only takes an hour or two and the cause of the problem is pretty apparent when the process is complete. Sadly, for most of these clients it's the first time they have ever done a budget. When I start asking questions they usually put up a fight, complaining that they don't have all the information they need, or they need their bookkeeper or accountant to help them. But I don't let them off the hook, because if I leave it to them it will rarely get done.

So, I assure them that all the information I need they will be able to give me off the top of their head. They usually give me a skeptical look but I just smile and start asking questions. The reasons my clients are so resistant to doing a budget are twofold. First, they think it is more complicated than it is, and secondly, they are afraid of what the budget will reveal.

Many small business owners, if not most, keep track of their business in their heads. They know, or think they know, from day to day where they stand both financially and operationally. Unfortunately, as the business gets more complicated these mental impressions are often false.

I tell them a budget is really quite simple. All they need to give me is an estimate of what revenue they have coming in each month and what expenses they expect to incur. As I pull up a simple spreadsheet on my computer, I start throwing out categories like sales receipts, advertising expense, travel, maintenance, and then record their answers. If they shrug and claim not to know, I make them give me a guess-timate which they can later verify. When the spreadsheet is printed out, it will usually reveal that their monthly cash outflow far exceeds their monthly receipts. This often shocks them, but just as often they just shrug like they knew this all along.

Gino shrugged when I told him his expenses exceeded

his income by nearly a thousand dollars a month. In his heart he knew it, but hadn't been able to face reality. He figured business would improve and eventually his income would catch up with his expenses. This was extremely unrealistic but a common belief among SBOs.

One of the problems I always face when dealing with SBOs is how to get paid. With money in short supply, paying an attorney is no easy trick. Gino offered me a custom suit in exchange for my help. It was the last thing I needed but I couldn't let down my very first client.

We wanted to set up a payment plan, but the landlord was threatening to lock Gino out, so we had to put them in Chapter 13 to protect them from a lockout. This worked out well and, after three tough years, Gino paid off all his creditors and life got back to normal. Gino and his family had survived and I was looking good in my custom-made Italian suits.

Even when I was able to get a client to acknowledge that he was looting his company, it wasn't always easy to get them to stop. I must confess I was guilty of looting my own law practice for many years. We were simply living above our means and the only source of revenue was the practice. I took what was needed to pay my personal bills, and there was nobody to tell me to stop.

When a business runs low on cash the natural thing to do is to borrow money. Unfortunately, this only makes matters worse as interest expense is added to the already overburdened budget, and eventually the borrowed money has to be repaid. Since bankers don't usually lend money to a business without collateral, the business owner now must pledge his assets and personally guarantee the indebtedness.

The only way out of this inevitable path to doom is extraordinary sales, unexpected windfalls, or wealthy relatives. Even if the small business owner is a great salesman or a gifted scientist, the lack of fundamental business acumen will eventually catch up with him.

This was the case with a computer genius, Sam Sturgeon. He had invented one of the first personal computers back in the eighties and had received a lot of good press. Sam, too, had made his employer very rich and decided he wanted some of that wealth for himself. His new line of computers were state of the art and selling like snow cones on a hot Sunday afternoon. He had a nice manufacturing plant in northwest Dallas with about twenty-five employees.

Six months later Sam came to see me about a Chapter 11. This is another form of bankruptcy utilized normally by corporations or partnerships. During the interview process I confirmed that he was indeed brilliant and quite a good salesman. He told me how well he had done and how much money he had made almost overnight. But when I compiled his financial statement he had virtually nothing. Then I discovered he'd been sponsoring a NASCAR racing team!

After shutting down his racing operation, we put his company in Chapter 11 and tried to reorganize. It was difficult case because he had waited too long to file and had virtually no cash. We did finally get his Chapter 11 confirmed, but while he was distracted by the bankruptcy, his competitors overtook him and he was never able to get back on top. Eventually he had to shut down.

It's not uncommon for someone who struggles for success and finally achieves it to think the battle is over and let down his guard. But the truth is, it's often harder to keep money than it is to earn it in the first place. The temptation to spend money sitting in a bank account or to let someone else spend it for you, is often so intense that only getting rid of it will once again bring peace.

A professional athlete was referred to me many years ago. He had come from a poor family and had been a neighborhood hero throughout high school and college. When he made it big in professional sports his family and friends decided he should open up a chain of restaurants. I was excited about seeing him because of his notoriety, but I was also anxious to help him get his business venture off to a good start.

Unfortunately, when he came in he was accompanied by his mother and several close friends. They were treating him like he was some kind of god and made it virtually impossible for me to talk candidly with him. As the meeting progressed, he told me of several loans to friends he was thinking about making and several joint ventures he was in the process of negotiating. Although he had a nice salary, he had no other assets. I cautioned him to take it slow and not get involved in a bunch of ventures he knew nothing about. His mother and friends became indignant and, needless to say, my services were quickly terminated.

A year or two later his career started going downhill and it wasn't long before he was out of the NBA. Although I don't know for sure, I suspect he has nothing left of the millions he received while playing in the NBA.

The point is, smart and talented business owners need to have a sound game plan just as much as the average ones. Brains and talent may prolong the date of business failure, but they won't prevent it.

The only way to stop looting a business is to set a modest, realistic salary that the business can easily support. Then at the end of the year, if there has been a profit and there is extra cash in the bank, the owner can take a bonus at that time. Conversely, if the business is still losing money, then the salary is too high and must be cut. This isn't to say that the business owner can't do other things to increase revenue or cut expenses, but until a profit is realized and there is extra cash in the bank, no bonuses should be declared.

I realize that often the salary a business can support is insufficient to meet the minimum needs of the owner. If this is the case, difficult decisions will have to be made. Perhaps the owner's spouse will have to get a job, or their lifestyle will have to be curtailed until the business is built up and can support a larger salary. The small business owner must be strong in this regard and avoid the temptation to loot the company. If this can't be done, then the sensible thing to do is shut down the business and go work for someone who can afford to pay you the big salary.

Chapter 3

Suffocation

In the euphoria of starting a new business, the temptation is to go first class. Unfortunately, first class is expensive. Most newly formed small businesses can't afford that kind of overhead, unless their business is a real cash cow, which is as rare as ozone over the North Pole. In the beginning, cash will be a precious commodity. This makes overhead extremely important because, if it is too high, the business will be in distress from day one.

You often hear that there are three important considerations in starting a business: location, location, and location. Too often the new business owner is obsessed with this principal and leases prime real estate for a three to five-year period at a cost the new business can't possibly support. By the time the business is up and running it is already in crisis. Each month cash flow is a major problem, distracting the owner from the critical needs of a new enterprise.

I remember a very bright entrepreneur who designed computer chips, Paul Blazer. For years he had a lucrative contract with TI, employed several other engineers, and was doing quite well—until the semi conductor industry went into a recession. His contract wasn't renewed, and there was little hope he could find new customers. Frustrated and depressed, he started looking for a new business. For whatever reason, he decided to open a restaurant. I told him the restaurant business wasn't a good choice as it required an experienced hand to be successful.

He just shrugged at this advice and said he had a new

concept that was sure to take off in a hurry. He wanted to open a restaurant that exclusively served salads. It was in the very beginning of the health craze that was sweeping the nation in late 80s and there wasn't anything like it at the time. When he brought a proposed lease to me, I gasped at the huge base rental. The lease also provided for the payment of a percentage of revenue over a fixed amount in addition to the base monthly rental. When I suggested he find a new location, he informed me he and his realtor had decided this was the *only* location that was suitable for his new restaurant. After all, location is everything.

Fortunately, it's not an attorney's job to be a mother. Sometimes I had to let my clients make mistakes, even if I knew in my heart it was a big one. Nevertheless, this was such a big mistake that I persisted in objecting to the cost of the lease and almost got fired. When the restaurant opened to much fanfare, I held my breath.

Needless to say, the restaurant didn't last six months, but it wasn't because the concept wasn't good. In fact, salad restaurants popped up all over the metroplex soon after my client's enterprise hit the bankruptcy court. From day one the overhead had been so high the restaurant had no chance of success.

In order for the typical under-capitalized small business to survive, overhead must be kept very modest such that a profit can still be made even when times are slow. This is why there are so many small, successful family run businesses opened up by new immigrants. Labor being the most expensive operating expense, they have an advantage because the family members perform most, if not all, of the labor for the business. These family members don't have to get a regular paycheck and often work for food, lodging, and a little spending money, while they go to school or look for other employment.

I recall getting a call once from a man who had opened

a Chinese restaurant, Don Chan. It was in a strip shopping center in a growing suburb of Dallas. It was his second restaurant but, unlike his first, he was compelled to staff the new restaurant with outside personnel since his family had its hands full with the first restaurant. Although business was okay, he had fallen behind on the rent and the landlord was threatening to lock him out. When Don came in and we looked at his finances more closely, I realized his business could never be successful because the rent and labor costs were too high. Even if we had filed a Chapter 11 it most likely wouldn't have been successful because the business couldn't make a profit given the rent and labor costs. He finally filed Chapter 7 and moved on.

Several months later I noticed that a Mexican restaurant had opened up in the same space in the shopping center. At the time I thought it was a very dangerous move since obviously this was a bad location for a restaurant. Curious about the new business, I had dinner there with my wife that night and introduced myself to the proud owner. In our conversation he acknowledged that most everyone operating the restaurant was family. The husband ran the wait staff, the wife did the cash register and some aunts and uncles handled the cooking. No doubt this new tenant got a better deal on the rent than the previous one, but I'm sure having much of his labor handled by family members was a significant factor in the new venture's success.

Ten years later we still eat at this restaurant at least once a week, and it just goes to show you that location isn't the only factor to consider in starting a new business. Overhead is as much of a consideration, if not greater.

Chapter 4

Starting On A Shoe String

As mentioned earlier, under-capitalization is a major cause of small business failure, particularly with so many chain stores and franchise operations muscling their way into almost every neighborhood. For some service businesses like a small law firm, insurance agency, realtor, or small accounting firm, capital isn't as critical as it is in other businesses. Some businesses, such as printers, small manufacturers, wholesalers, or auto repair shops require extensive furniture, equipment and inventory. For the latter, starting with adequate capitalization is critical for their survival.

· Today I have two clients in the wholesale distribution business who are both quite successful—JB Gift Distributors and Addison Electric. But their success came only after first failing because they were inadequately capitalized. Both owners had learned their trade while working for other similar companies. After a while they believed they had the expertise to run their own companies, so they ventured out by themselves. Lacking capital they borrowed heavily to purchase the large inventories they needed to start business. This was the mid-80s just before the economy collapsed. At first they did well, but when the savings and loan crisis hit, only to be followed by a recession, they were caught short of capital. One of the banks called in JB's loan and Addison got way behind with vendors and the IRS. Both companies ended up in bankruptcy, one in Chapter 7 and the other in Chapter 11.

JB filed Chapter 11 in the fall. Fortunately most of its debts were to suppliers and the IRS rather than large banks or financial institutions, which are much harder to deal with because they are secured creditors and have greater rights than priority or unsecured creditors. The only complication was a creditor's committee that was led by the largest unsecured creditor, a supplier who would take a big hit if the plan were confirmed as proposed. The creditor opposed nearly everything we did, but eventually realized that getting something was better than nothing. We settled by agreeing to pay twenty-five cents on the dollar rather than ten percent we initially proposed. By the next summer, its plan was confirmed and JP came out of bankruptcy. It was successful only because seventy-five percent of its debt was eliminated in the reorganization, overhead was slashed, and the government and secured creditors were forced to restructure the debts owed them and accept a long-term payout.

Addison Electric started over. They owed a large sum to a bank and were way behind in lease payments, but had kept their suppliers paid. This would have made a Chapter 11 difficult because the bank and the landlord would have required payment in full, and they wouldn't have to agree to a long-term payout. So the owner of Addison Electric, a high-roller with a high maintenance wife, started over this time with a lot more capital, less overhead, and the knowledge learned from his first venture into the small business arena.

He vowed not to make the same mistakes he had made the first time around and, with his client base intact, took off fast without much capitalization. Today he calls on me for estate and tax planning issues more than anything else. His business is growing rapidly and now is worth millions. But he was only able to launch his new distribution business because he had a client base established. He was lucky in this regard, because an astute Chapter 7 trustee would have recognized the value of his client base and tried to sell it rather than abandoning it to the SBO debtor. Fortunately for him, most

Chapter 7 trustees are so busy and overburdened that they rarely go after an intangible asset like goodwill. They tend to focus on hard assets like vehicles, inventory, equipment, and accounts receivable. In this case, the trustee never even considered the most valuable asset of all, a list of over five hundred active clients who ordered electrical parts and supplies almost every week.

So why do entrepreneurs start a business when they know that they don't have enough capital? Is it overconfidence, unrealistic optimism, or stupidity? My observation is that it is all of the above, plus a denial of reality. I remember when I got out of college and started looking for a job, how helpless and frustrated I felt going from one prospective employer to another trying to sell myself and land a job. It was demeaning, humiliating, and I hated it. It wasn't long before I vowed to own my own business so I didn't have to kiss anyone's ass. When I got out of law school, I didn't even apply for a job with a big law firm, because I didn't want to have to interview and beg for a position. Once the seeds of independence are sown, nothing can stop them from growing into an independent spirit.

I didn't realize it until years later, but my life was predestined by my parents and my circumstances when I was a child. Being a little overweight and introverted like my father, I didn't have a lot of friends and never learned to socialize very well. My self-esteem was pretty low, and it wasn't until high school that I discovered I wasn't as dumb as everybody thought. I'm not sure exactly what triggered this realization, but it was too late as my shy, introverted personality had already set and couldn't be easily changed.

Because Mr. Popularity, I wasn't, I had to learn to be independent and self-motivated. In the short run it was pretty depressing as I envied all the popular, socially skilled kids that got all the attention and respect. In later years I was glad I had learned to survive on my own without depending on others—particularly as clients paraded through my office every day, the victims of corporate maneuvering or indiscretions.

If being an entrepreneur is a conscious choice, as I am sure it is for some, the reasons for being independent are many. Some see it as the only way to have a chance at becoming rich and famous. Why work to make someone else wealthy, I often hear them say. Others have great dreams and aspirations that they feel will never be obtained if someone else controls their destiny. These entrepreneurs often become obsessed with making their dreams a reality, so that they often overlook or ignore the obvious risks and pitfalls that lay before them. They simply don't care about reality. In their minds somehow they will overcome the odds and achieve success. It's a tragic case of self-deception. So many entrepreneurs start off their new businesses keenly aware that they are grossly under-capitalized, but believing firmly that somehow they will survive and be successful.

Chapter 5

Giving It Away

Another big cause of small business failure, particularly in the construction industry, is bidding the job so low that there is no way a profit could possibly be made. This usually occurs when there is competition for the job and the small business owner desperately needs the work. It's a very common practice in the construction business to borrow from Peter to pay Paul. It works like this.

The owner bids the job too low and then runs out of money to complete it. Rather than default on the project, get sued, and be put out of business, he runs out and gets another job. With the up-front money on the new job, he completes the old one. This will work for awhile, but eventually the contractor either won't be able to get a new job quickly enough, or the up-front money he gets on the second job isn't sufficient to finish the first job.

This is when I usually get the phone calls and confessions from my construction clients that they have underbid and job and can't finish it. Before they call me, they have usually exhausted any possibility of getting a new job or borrowing the money. By this time the customer is belligerent and may have contacted an attorney. This is when I usually suggest Chapter 13 because that normally that solves the problem in short order. Unlike Chapter 7, there are no provisions in the laws governing Chapter 13 cases that allow a creditor to object to a plan on the grounds of fraud or intentional wrongdoing. The only objection that can be raised is that the Chapter 13 was brought in bad faith. In most cases, however, even if the debtor has fraudulently taken money from a creditor, he is likely filing the Chapter 13 with every intention of making it work. Hence an objection by the wronged creditor won't stop his Chapter 13 case from proceeding. As effective as Chapter 13 is at saving the hide of imprudent contractors, it doesn't stop criminal prosecution.

Several years ago I got a frantic phone call from a contractor who had underbid a string of jobs and was at the end of the line. Unfortunately, this last owner hired an astute attorney who knew that what the contractor had done was not only fraudulent, but violated a Texas criminal statute. He knew the contractor didn't have any money and probably couldn't pay a judgment, so he had his client file criminal charges. My client was flabbergasted because he didn't see himself as a criminal. After all, what he had done was pretty common practice among his peers. But the owner and his attorney wouldn't back off, and the District Attorney pressed on with the criminal prosecution.

Terrified of the prospect of going to jail, my client begged his family and friends to bail him out and they did. With money in hand we offered it to the owner with the stipulation that he would sign a non-prosecution affidavit. He agreed and my client tendered the money. This didn't guarantee that the DA would dismiss the case, but normally they will if the plaintiff asks them to and there has been restitution.

So, the question is: Why do contractors underbid a job? Many times it is done inadvertently, because either the owner or the estimator doesn't understand how to determine the total costs of doing a job, or is overly optimistic in calculating the time it will take to get it done.

Bidding a job is very complicated and easy to botch. Many contractors don't keep books or do any kind of cost accounting, so they really don't know how much it costs to complete a job. Oftentimes they fail to take into consideration administrative costs, depreciation of equipment, interest expense, taxes, and other expenses that don't seem directly related to the project.

Another big problem with bidding a job is being overly optimistic. Contractors often seem to think it will take less time to finish a job than it actually does. They may underestimate the cost or quantity of materials needed or fail to consider the likelihood of price increases. Whereas these SBOs usually do quality work, they very often totally miscalculate the bid and end up in serious trouble.

The solution is to keep a good set of books with accurate cost accounting so that the business owner will know exactly what his or her costs are. Then, when the bid is calculated, a little profit can be built in to make the whole exercise worthwhile. The owner must resist the temptation to bid the job below cost or with too little profit just to keep busy. If he can't do this he should turn over the bidding process to someone more objective and who has strict instructions to bid the job strictly on a cost plus reasonable profit basis. Whereas the owner is usually the person with the best knowledge of how to do the job, he may be the worst person to bid it.

Underbidding a job is crazy and totally avoidable, at least the second time around. The first time it might be an honest mistake, but after that it's stupidity. If the owner bids the job correctly and doesn't get the job, then he has to be able to just shrug it off and go on to the next one. If he bids correctly, but doesn't get any jobs, then he must look at ways to cut his costs or improve his efficiency so he can do the job for less money. But he must be realistic. Just getting a job for the sake of getting it is foolish and an invitation for disaster.

Plastic

They came from everywhere
Over here and over there
The mail, the phone, the mall
Unsolicited, one and all
Get them one, two, or ten
Don't wait—pick up the pen

It's a simply wonderful game
All you do is sign your name
Now jump for joy, and yell hooray!
Cause baby they're on their way
Dillards, Penneys to name a few
Visa, Mastercard, and Amex Blue

You can live the American dream
Stand up now and let out a scream
Buy it now, no money down
You've got credit all over town
Sit back and watch your dreams come true
Don't worry, only pennies due

For Moses it was manna provided by the Lord
No need to sit around the house so bored
Now its silver, gold, and platinum too
Macy's, Sears to name just two
Cars, clothes, a ten day cruise
Gambling, clubs, and lots of booze

You've got it all and then some more
Until the bills flood in the door
It cannot be, I didn't spend that much
Just a few odds and ends and such
Eighteen, twenty, twenty-four
Interest, interest, bills galore

Oh my God, it's all a scam
To steal my life, I'm in a jam
Collectors call day and night
My balances are out of sight
I can't sleep or think
Go to work, eat or drink

My lover scorns me, yells, and screams
God, what happened to my dreams?
Letters come demanding blood,
Tears from my face do flood
My lovers's gone, couldn't take the heat
I'm here alone, tired and beat

Is all that's left bankruptcy?
What was my sin? Idolatry
I see it now, clear as glass
I fell in love with cold, hard cash
Visa, Mastercard, Amex Blue
Lucifer got his due

Chapter 6

The Credit Conspiracy

From the day you are born you are indoctrinated on how important credit is to everyone. You're told over and over again that good credit is the secret to financial success and happiness in life. You're barraged with advertisements for all the expensive luxury items you can buy right now on credit and nearly everyone takes the bait.

You get a house you can't afford, a luxury car you don't need, and run up a half-dozen credit cards to the hilt. Before you know it you're a slave to the system. Most of your hard-earned money is going to banks and mortgage companies in interest payments. You pay and pay and pay, yet the balance you owe never goes down. Soon the joy is gone in your life—happiness is replaced with constant worry and depression.

Yes, from the day we are born, each and every one of us have been carefully manipulated into becoming slaves. Yes, carefully programmed robots who go to work everyday and then religiously send seventy to eighty percent of our wealth to our masters, the big corporate giants of Wall Street and the government bureaucrats in Washington.

Think about it. From the day you are born you're told that good credit is your ticket to the American dream. You can have all the luxuries and modern conveniences of life on credit. Why wait, they say, when you can have it right now.

Let's say you're a middle class family with annual income of forty thousand dollars a year. If you work forty years you'll earn 1.6 million dollars. If you're a typical family you'll buy a hundred and fifty thousand dollar home, a car every six or seven years, and have a half dozen credit cards maxed out very early in the game.

Now the enemy here is compound interest. It's common knowledge you will pay nearly triple the amount financed over thirty years. For instance you'll pay $415,213 over thirty years for that $150,000 home at 8.5%. The cars will cost at least twenty-five percent more than their initial cost, and you'll be paying the minimums on your credit cards until you're dead and buried. Now if you subtract twenty-five percent of your income for taxes that leaves you with $1,200,000. Subtract $415,000 for what you actually pay for your home, including all the interest, and now you only have $750,000. By the time you take away $200,000 or so for your automobiles you have only $585,000 left to live on for 40 years!

This is less than $15,000 a year for food, clothing, utilities, insurance, gasoline, home and auto maintenance, medical expenses, recreation, entertainment, education, vacations, and retirement. It's no wonder the average person is broke all the time—barely making ends meet! It's no wonder it takes two breadwinners nowadays to survive. It's no wonder the divorce rate has gone to the roof and teenage suicides are at a historical high.

Millions of Americans, including myself, have been victimized by this credit conspiracy. The lure of easy money is so tantalizing that few can resist it. I started my own law practice with a two-thousand dollar cash advance on my American Express card. I tried to get conventional financing but had no collateral, so I was summarily turned down. Over the years I continued to finance my small business with high-interest credit card debt that I had no prayer of ever paying off.

A lot of small business are started and financed with credit cards each year this same way. A few will be successful and pay off this high-cost debt, but most will eventually perish because of it. Eventually the burden of the minimum monthly payments will get so heavy that the business will collapse. I remember one bankruptcy client who had charged a whopping $150,000 on eleven credit cards from the same financial institution to fund his poorly run business. It amazed me that company had let him have eleven cards in the first place, but the fact that he was able to run up $150,000 in debt was mind boggling. During the course of the bankruptcy I fully expected this creditor to come up with some kind of a objection to the bankruptcy but we never heard from them.

Credit cards are very handy and useful for travel and to make it easy to keep track of business expenses. But they shouldn't be used for financing your business or covering your negative cash flow at home. If you are using credit cards for this purpose you need to stop immediately and take a close look at the business. Find out what is wrong and correct it, but don't keep digging a hole that will eventually swallow you and your small business.

The Banker

If you borrow money
You should be aware
Of the truth about some bankers
Lest you fall into their snare

Interest is their magic wand
That brings them mighty riches
Keep a careful eye on it
Or you'll lose your frickin' britches

Stacks and stacks of papers
They'll thrust into your face
Hoping you won't read them
Cause the loan's a damn disgrace

They'll want your guarantee
Your aunt's and uncle's too
And a pledge of all your assets
I guess, that'll have to do

They'll treat you like a king at first
Smile, pat you on the back
Until something goes awry
Or falls into a crack

Then they'll call you twice a day
To find out what's gone wrong
Gotta have that payment soon
Can't wait, it's been too long

If you ask them for more time
They'll frown and say "no way."
Gotta get the payment now
Can't wait another day

As they haul your assets off
You'll scream and yell in vain
Now that you've got nothin'
You can barely stand the pain

So, now the truth I've told you
Keep a sharp and wary eye
'Cause the thing about your banker
He's slick and very sly

Chapter 7

Greedy Lenders

In many businesses, financing is absolutely necessary. For instance, doctors and dentists require a lot of expensive equipment to operate their practices. A trucking company or car rental agency obviously will have to finance their vehicles. If your small business requires any kind of financing be careful. Bankers are a greedy bunch, and you will pay dearly for the money you have to borrow. Not only will the interest and fees be outrageous, but they will also want you to pledge every asset you own to secure their loan to you.

The key to negotiating a good loan is not to need the money. Most SBOs wait until they are in desperate need of cash before they go to their banker. Without batting an eye they sign anything their banker sticks in front of them. They rarely read the voluminous paperwork associated with the loan and hardly ever get the advice of an attorney. Few realize how much power they have given to the cold, arrogant banker who cares nothing about them, but only about the big profits his bank will be making off your sweat.

When I read through commercial loan documentation today I am appalled at how the finance industry is taking advantage of the SBO. Not only do banks require far too much collateral, but it is common now for banks to make a borrower waive all defenses and offsets that they might have against the bank, waive the right to a jury trial, waive notice of default, comply with highly complex financial ratios that few of them understand, provide burdensome financial reporting and documentation, and even sign over the business to the bank before they will make the loan.

Borrowing money today is almost as dangerous as smoking cigarettes or sniffing cocaine. The SBO may not die from borrowing money, but his business could be snatched away from him in a heartbeat. As soon as he signs the big stack of loan documents his future is in grave danger. In fact, I've found many, if not most, small business loans are in default before the ink is dry. If you read all the onerous provisions and requirements of these documents, few SBOs could ever comply with them. Consequently, the banker has the power to put you out of business at will.

If you make every payment on time you might be okay, but almost every small business owner has cash flow crunches from time and time. Once your payment to the bank gets behind, your business is in serious jeopardy. Whereas some bankers will cut you some slack, just as many won't care about your plight and will pull the choke chain and you'll be out of business.

So what do you do if you absolutely must have capital for your business. First of all, it's far better to get investors than borrow money. You would be surprised at how many of your friends and family would be willing to invest in your business if you would ask them. Investor money doesn't have to be paid back and doesn't accrue interest. This gives the investor financed business a great competitive advantage in the marketplace.

For instance, the publishing business is a brutally competitive business today. If you walk into any major chain bookstore and look around you will be overwhelmed by the number of titles you have to choose from.. The big publishing houses spend hundreds of thousands of dollars to promote many of their front line titles. They have big sales forces and often purchase exclusive use of the prime shelf space in the bookstores.

For someone to start a small press in this environment might seem foolhardy, but it is done every day. The SBO in this case has investor money, or is putting up his own money to finance the business. If he had to borrow money, he wouldn't last six months because very little revenue comes in during the first six months of operations in this industry. Even after that, revenue growth is slow, so it's imperative to have a very low overhead.

Those who invest in small businesses are simply betting on the ability of the SBO to make the business a success. Over the years I have helped a number of fortunate SBOs sell their businesses for over a million of dollars. Had these ventures been financed by investment capital rather than commercial loans, the investors would have made a killing. I know of one such investor who has now retired and spends half his time in his million dollar home in Dallas and the other half of his time in his million dollar beach house in Maui.

If you can't find any investors, try to get unsecured loans if possible. It's amazing how much money can be borrowed today without putting up collateral. Every week I get applications in the mail for $25-100,000 unsecured lines of credit. If you have good credit so you can do this and not pay too high an interest rate, then that is the way to go.

If you can't get an unsecured loan, then the next best thing is a loan without recourse. This means your collateral is at risk but the bank can't come after you personally for any deficiency they suffer. In real estate financing I see this type of financing all the time, particularly by life insurance companies. If the bank is anxious to make the loan they might agree to do this if you ask for it. If they say "no," thank them and keep looking. When they see that the non-recourse financing is a deal-breaker, they might change their mind. If not, you're better off to keep looking.

You should always try to avoid personal guarantees. If

your business is doing well and has accumulated assets, then it should be able to borrow money on its own financial statement. Why should you have to risk every dime you've earned over the years? Don't give in to your banker's insistence that you personally guarantee every loan.

Preparation for obtaining a loan is very important. Before you apply for a loan, you should get with your attorney and set up what I call a defensive estate plan. What this means is that you structure your assets in such a way that they aren't vulnerable to all the predators lurking about who are looking for an opportunity to take them away from you. This is done by setting up a living trust to provide you with a little privacy and a layer of insulation from your predators.

A living trust is simply another legal entity which you control that holds most of your assets. One of the great advantages is the privacy that it provides both while you are alive and if you or your spouse should die. When you give someone a financial statement, all you have to disclose is the value of the living trust ownership interest. There is no requirement that you itemize each asset held in the trust. People may ask you to disclose the trust holdings, but it is your option whether or not to do it. My recommendation is to hold your assets close to your vest. The less the rest of the world knows, the better.

Once everything is in your living trust, it then sets up a family limited partnership. A family limited partnership is simply a limited partnership of the SBO and his living trust, or sometimes a corporate general partner and the SBO's living trust. The FLP, as it's called, provides additional privacy, some tax advantages, but most of all, asset protection. This is because most limited partnership statutes do not allow a creditor to seize assets from a FLP, but only to surcharge the partner's interest. This makes it very difficult for a predator to successfully steal assets from an SBO.

Once you have set up your defensive estate plan, you'll want to keep your financial affairs private and only tell lenders as little as possible about the assets you have. Remember, your banker will want every asset he knows about as collateral. You have no obligation to tell him what is in your FLP because it is not borrowing the money. If the banker won't lend you what you want without knowing what's in the FLP, go to another bank.

The key to getting a loan on your terms is not to be desperate. Be prepared to walk away if the bank isn't willing to make the loan documents fair and reasonable. Don't agree to guarantee the loan and only give them a reasonable amount of collateral. If the lender wants to make the loan, they will bend to your will. If they won't be reasonable, find another lender.

The Bookkeeper

Sally Ann, that was her name
Pretty and bright, she knew the game
Bookkeeping, typing—she did it all
She lifted our load so we'd stand tall

Happy, relieved we'd found what we sought
We left her alone, scarcely gave her a thought
She was in early each day, left late at night
A hard worker she was, what a delight!

A year went by then cash got so tight
We shuddered to think of our horrible plight
Plenty of business, we all worked hard
Then it hit us, we'd let down our guard

Money is missing, where did it go?
We asked Sally Ann, she said, "I don't know."
Shocked and dismayed at this twist of fate
We poured over the books until very late

Then we saw it, the game she had played
Anger swept o'er us, we had been betrayed
We called our attorney, the sheriff, the DA
She couldn't get away with it, she had to pay

But alas, she was smart and vanished that night
Gone away, far away by dawn's early light
Leaving us reeling, depressed, without hope
Wondering if we'd reached the end of the rope?

Chapter 8

Theft and Embezzlement

A critical problem for SBO is finding people they can trust. Nobody can watch every employee every minute. There are a myriad of ways customers and employees can steal from you without being detected. Such was the case for Don and Ho Park, who brought their life's savings from Korea and opened up a janitorial business in Arlington. They felt fortunate when a bright young woman answered their ad for a bookkeeper. She was kind and patient with them and helped them master the English language. She seemed to know all the ins and outs of accounting, payroll and tax compliance, so they left all those matters in her hands. Her salary wasn't cheap but it was reasonable considering all that she did for them.

Business started out slow but grew steadily for several years as they acquired more and more customers. Even though sales were good and overhead was modest, they seemed to always have cash flow problems. Since they didn't understand financial statements or bookkeeping they had no idea what was happening to them. Finally they started watching the bookkeeper a little more carefully and noticed the deposits she was making were for less than the receipts they were giving her. When confronted with this she confessed that she routinely took ten percent from each deposit and put it into her account. Over the years it had amounted to more than $50,000!

Don and Ho were shocked and horrified by this betrayal. When I suggested they go to the DA, however, they declined because as they were so humiliated by what happened and didn't want anyone to know about it. I understood how they felt but didn't relish the idea of letting the bookkeeper off the hook so easily. Eventually, Don and Ho were able to pull themselves out of the huge hole that their employee had dug for them, but only because they were running a tight ship and had a lot of friends and family providing a cheap labor pool. A more marginal business wouldn't have been able to survive a $50,000 hit like they did.

There are other, more creative ways to embezzle which are difficult to detect. In a case in Desoto, a convenience store had been in operation for years when the owner, Pete Briggs, decided to move to the country. He turned over the business to a manager who had been with him for several years and he trusted implicitly. Over the next eighteen months or so he discovered his sales were down and wondered what was going on, since business had always been good at this store. When the manager was confronted about the shortage and poor sales he just shrugged and said times were bad.

Later when Peter asked his accountant about the losses, he told him that there was a serious inventory shortage. At this point we were hired to try to get to the bottom of the problem. When we started interviewing employees we discovered that the manager had systematically fired all the old employees and hired members of his own family to work in the store. He also conveniently disabled all the security cameras and claimed they were being repaired.

After inspecting cash register tapes we discovered that there were hundreds of voided transactions, which we suspected meant sales were being made, the tickets voided, and the money pocketed. Unfortunately, when we subpoenaed bank records, we couldn't find any extra cash coming into the account. Since all the employees were related to the manager, they were uncooperative in our investigation. The only explanation we could come up with was that the manager was spending all the money that he was stealing. This certainly was possible, but there was a quarter million dollars missing, so we were pretty sure there must be a stash somewhere.

When we took the deposition of the manager's spouse, we discovered she had her own small landscape business. The business seemed legitimate until we tried to find out who her customers were. She could only name a few and was very vague as to the jobs she had under contract. It soon became clear that the money being embezzled by her husband was being booked as the sales for her landscape business.

In going through her bank statements with her, I noticed several large withdrawals. When I asked her about them, she claimed it was her practice to withdraw large sums to purchase cashiers checks to pay bills. When I pointed out that on several occasions there were no cashier's checks purchased, she admitted to storing the cash in her freezer until she needed it.

During all this time the DA couldn't be bothered with the prosecution of an embezzlement case because he felt it would be too difficult to prove. Eventually the case settled and the client recovered $100,000 of the quarter million embezzlement. Fortunately for my client, his business had a prime location, so he was able to sell his business and recoup his money, but his was a unique case. Most SBOs couldn't survive a quarter million dollar embezzlement, and I know of several who had to file bankruptcy after losing far less than that.

I could go on and on with more tales of employee dishonesty as it is very common. The point I want to make is that employee dishonesty usually occurs because the SBO is not paying close enough attention to his business. Employee's should be carefully screened before they are hired. Resumes should be verified, criminal background checks should be made, and references checked.

Once employees are hired, it's not wise to trust all of the accounting to one person. More than one employee should handle deposits, check-writing, and checkbook reconciliations. Spread the work around to make it difficult for one person to control the system. The owner should always review bank statements for irregularities. Monthly profit and loss statements should be created and routinely reviewed to spot unusual entries or trends. Blank checks should never be written.

I had one client who would routinely sign blank checks whenever she was out of town or on vacation. Her bookkeeper would then pay the bills as they came in. After a few years, when cash flow began to be a problem, the owner started to review her old bank statements. To her shock, she found she had been double paying vendors. When she checked with the vendors they denied being paid twice. Upon checking with the bank, it seems the bookkeeper had set up accounts with names similar to the vendor's and was depositing the extra check into her own accounts.

Usually the bank will have to make good on checks they accept with forged signatures, but in this case it was not that simple. The signatures were valid and the bank alleged that our client was negligent in signing blank checks. On the other hand, the endorsements were fraudulent and we alleged that the bank was negligent in letting this employee set up all these bank accounts in fictitious names. The dispute went into litigation which lasted for years. Eventually the case settled and our client got partial restitution, but the battle cost my client dearly in time, money, and mental distress.

In fact, the woman who had written the blank checks felt so guilty that she became obsessed with the case, calling me every day and sometimes several times a day about it. She wanted the money that she lost, but more than that, she wanted the bookkeeper to pay. The case was so distracting and mentally debilitating to her that she could scarcely work in the business after this happened.

Your accountant can recommend other measures to

protect against employee dishonesty, and these measures should always be implemented. Many people blame their accountant for not detecting embezzlement, but usually the employee is smart enough to hide their handiwork so that the accountant won't readily see it. It's the SBO who has the best shot at detecting dishonesty, because he or she is there every day and should detect any irregularities.

If all else fails, the SBO can get fidelity insurance to cover any losses suffered from employee dishonesty. Generally the insurance is inexpensive and can be attached as a rider to a general liability policy. The sad thing I've found, however, is that very few SBOs have this type of insurance coverage.

Chapter 9

Competition

Competition is a major contributor to small business failure. When the big chain store or franchise operation moves in down the street, it's just a matter of time before the small business folds. The big chain and franchise stores buy in bigger quantities, which allows them to undercut the prices charged by the small business owners. They have much larger reserves and can keep prices low until they put you out of business. The only defense against this is to run a tight operation and provide better and more personal services to your customers so they will be willing to pay a little more for your product. Customer loyalty takes time to build, but when it is finally achieved, it can provide stability and insulation from competitive forces.

But what I want to concentrate on are those types of competition that you can guard against and do something about should they threaten your small business. These practices are called "unfair competition," and they can literally destroy a small business overnight. They include libel and slander, personnel raiding, breach of confidentiality, dissemination of trade secrets, interference with contract, and price-fixing.

Recently I got a call from a client who was in the consulting business. The client was very upset because a salesmen in a competitive business was telling the client's existing and potential customers that they had infringed on the competitor's copyright. It was a lie and an obvious attempt to subvert the business relationship of the parties. If this type of slander were allowed to go unanswered, our client would no doubt have lost that customer and maybe the business.

Our response was to send a cease-and-desist letter advising the competitor that our client was prepared to go to court should they persist in slandering our client. In most cases this will stop the unfair business practice but, if it doesn't, it's important to follow through with your threats and seek a temporary injunction. Once the competitor knows you are serious about protecting your rights, they will usually back off.

A more subtle attack on a small business is theft of employees. Almost every business will have one or more key employees who are instrumental to the success of the business. They might be sales representative, technical personnel, or administrators. The competition soon learns who these people are and will start plotting a way to steal them from you. And if it isn't the competition, often it's one of these employees themselves who suddenly realize they are the key to the business' success. So they decide to go out on their own, expecting to get rich themselves rather than make an ungrateful employer rich.

Invariably these key people will try to take others with them. The loss of one or two key employees like this can devastate a business and quickly put it in jeopardy. Luckily, this is a danger that can be easily avoided simply by having properly drafted employment contracts with these key people. These should be drafted carefully by an attorney and include appropriate non-competition, non-solicitation, and non-disclosure agreements. Typically these key employees will be prohibited from going into business in the same territory for several years after their termination, prohibited from soliciting employees from the business for this period, and prohibited from disclosing any proprietary information or trade secrets learned during their employment.

Theft of proprietary information and trade secrets is another way a small business can be placed in jeopardy. I once represented a software engineer who was employed by a video game company. While employed by the company, the engineer developed video game technology that was state of the art and very valuable. Although the company had paid him everything he was due under his employment contract, he realized how valuable his technology had become and was bitter that he didn't own it. Fortunately for the company, they had a good employment contract which stipulated that any technology developed for the company belonged to the company.

Nevertheless, the employee felt like it was his technology and decided to quit and take the technology to a competitor who would pay him a handsome sum for it. If the employer had allowed this to happen, they not only would have lost the technology, but their competitor would have been in a position to bury them. Because they had properly documented their ownership of the technology, they were able to file a complaint for theft of a trade secret with the District Attorney. This is when I was hired by the employee, who was about to go to jail.

I explained to him that when he accepted employment with his employer, he had sold any rights to anything he developed while being employed by the company. He was bitter because he claimed the owners had promised him stock options, bonuses, and other fringe benefits that they hadn't delivered. This may well have been true, but none of those things were in the employment contract he had signed. I told him his mistake was signing an employment contract without advice of counsel.

A few days later I arranged an informal negotiation session to try to resolve the dispute. It was a very tense and bitter meeting as both parties had a lot at stake. Finally, we reached a compromise whereby the engineer would get a nice, 90-day severance package to give him time to find a new job, the employer would sign a non-prosecution agreement, and the engineer would acknowledge the company's ownership of the technology. As we were driving away, the engineer let out a sigh of relief. I turned and smiled at him. He said he was glad they had settled, because if they hadn't he was prepared to put them out of business. When I asked him how he could have done that, he said that before he left the company he had sabotaged all the company's computers. He pulled a remote control device from his pocket and waived it in front of me. Then he smiled and said, "Push this little button and BOOM! It would be all over."

Chapter 10

Misfortune

No small business owner is immune from misfortune. Eventually it will strike. It always does. Fortunately, misfortune can usually be anticipated, and plans can be made to mitigate its impact. Yet many SBOs totally ignore the risks and dangers inherent in running a business and fail to take any measures to protect themselves.

The worst blow to any small business is the loss of the owner or a key employee. Yet very few small businesses have adequate life and disability insurance on these key figures. If there is insurance, it is purchased to protect the spouse or children with little thought to what would be necessary to preserve the business itself.

Another common omission is contents insurance. Whereas the landlord usually insures his building, the tenant often doesn't bother to take out a contents policy. If a fire occurs and his business assets are destroyed, he may have no recourse and find himself out of business. Even if the tenant does have contents insurance, rarely is there business interruption insurance. After a fire, a business may be shut down for months and, without income for that period, most businesses will fail or be forced into bankruptcy.

I can remember two of my clients who suffered this fate. One was an immigrant from China who had established a very nice computer training school in North Dallas. His training was state-of- the-art and in high demand. Unfortunately, one night there was a fire in his office building. When he went to work he found his business totally destroyed.

He had bought fire insurance to replace his computers and equipment, but had very limited business interruption coverage. When he finally got the proceeds from his insurance it wasn't enough to pay even half the debts he had racked up while he was shut down.

Another client owned a very popular independent grocery store in the mid-cities area. He had owned the store for years, and it made a very nice living for him, his wife and several family members. One night he was called and advised that his store was on fire. When he got there, his heart sank as most of the store was gutted. Although he had adequate fire insurance, he didn't have business interruption insurance. As the months dragged, his customers found other places to buy groceries. Because he had gone almost six months without income, he had exhausted all his capital and, when he reopened to lackluster sales, he was forced into Chapter 11. He struggled for six months to come up with a viable plan but ultimately had to convert to Chapter 7.

Another danger to SBOs is employees. Employees have a propensity for being injured on the job and expect the employer to take care of them until they recover, even if it was their own fault they were injured. The workman's compensation system was developed to protect the employer from this potentially devastating liability, but over the years the cost of workman's compensation insurance has become cost prohibitive in the eyes of many SBOs. Because of this, many SBOs have elected to opt out of the system and go naked or provide an alternate plan to deal with on-the-job injuries.

Most of these alternative plans do not provide anywhere near the protection that a regular workman's compensation policy would provide. Consequently, many SBOs facing substantial employee claims can be literally put out of business because the law provides that without workman's compensation coverage, all common law defenses the employer would normally have are lost.

Another pitfall that SBOs often stumble into is terminating employees while on workman's compensation or with an outstanding claim for an on-the-job injury. It's often difficult for an employer to continue to pay an employee who has been injured and can't perform his or her job. I frequently receive calls from my clients asking if they can terminate an injured employee, particularly if it is clear he would never be able to resume his job. I have to tell them they can't do this because injured employees are protected by law, and employers can be sued if they wrongfully terminate an employee. This is extremely frustrating to my clients and difficult for them to accept.

It is particularly bad when the employer thinks the employee has faked the injury. One client, a rather outspoken owner of a chain of dry cleaners in Dallas called me one Monday morning and said an employee had reported an injury while bending down to pick up a basket of clothing. The employee reported that as he straightened up he felt something pull in his back and felt a sharp pain. Of course there were no witnesses to this injury, and my client was convinced the injury took place over the weekend while the employee was gardening at home. Apparently a coworker had heard the employee talking to someone on the phone, remarking that he had injured himself while gardening the day before.

When my client heard of this, he got very angry and fired the employee. Unfortunately, the coworker who heard the admission was an illegal immigrant and was afraid to testify. It wasn't long before my client was served with a lawsuit for wrongful termination. The lawyer who handled the case for the employee specialized in this area and took all his cases on a contingent-fee basis. The law was so much in favor of the employee that this attorney found it a very lucrative business to prey on SBOs struggling to keep their labor costs down.

Although insurance against all of these hazards isn't cheap, it's not usually all that expensive either. In the long run, it's much cheaper to have the insurance than to suffer the consequences of having no coverage at all. SBOs are an optimistic bunch and often delude themselves into thinking disaster won't strike them. But they are wrong; it's just a matter of time until it strikes everyone.

Chapter 11

Larger Forces

So far I've talked about avoidable causes of small business failure. Unfortunately, sometimes there are larger forces at work over which the small business owner has no control. These are events and occurrences for which there is no insurance and no strategy that is likely to save them.

One such event happened to the same client whose store was gutted by a fire. After it was apparent he couldn't reopen the business, he took the proceeds of his business and bought another grocery store in East Texas. For several years the store did very well, and he and his family were again making a comfortable living. Then one day he read in the newspaper that Walmart was building a store less than a half mile away.

A year later he had to file Chapter 11 again. It was very sad but there was nothing he could have done to avoid this eventuality. In the mid-80s many of my clients suffered a similar fate as a result of the bank and savings and loan crisis. Thousands of loans that were being paid in a timely fashion were suddenly called in. Credit lines that were the life blood of other businesses were abruptly cut off. Stunned business owners suddenly found themselves having to scrape together large sums of money or face their banker in court. The ones who couldn't raise the necessary cash were forced to shut down their business or file for bankruptcy protection.

Unfortunately, I don't know of any way to protect yourself against these larger forces that can overwhelm a small business owner at any time. The events of September 11, 2001 certainly couldn't have been anticipated. There is little a single SBO can do when these cataclysmic events take place. Accordingly, I don't intend to deal with that type of catastrophe in this book. My emphasis will be to concentrate on the more common issues, the avoidable pitfalls that every small business owner can protect himself against.

PART 2

FIGHTING FOR SURVIVAL

Chill, It's No Big Deal

Get a nasty letter in the mail?
Send us money or we'll give you hell?
Don't lose your cool, don't get upset
Chill, it's no big deal

Creditor called and wants his bread?
Got to have it now, no more said?
Don't get upset, don't be depressed
Chill, it's no big deal

Constable come knocking at your door?
You've been sued, can't take no more?
Take a deep breath, don't despair
Chill, it's no big deal

Didn't pay your taxes? Owe a lot?
Accounts been seized. Now your checks are hot?
Take a walk, get some air
Chill, it's no big deal

Rent is late? Landlord lookin' for the cash?
Wants the rent or you're out on your ass
Take two aspirin and go to bed
Chill, it's no big deal

'Cause when your world starts to crumble
Your lawyer will be sure you don't stumble
He'll smile as he takes your cash and tell you
Chill, it's no big deal

Chapter 12

It's Not As Bad As It Looks

Before I discuss the fundamentals of successfully operating a small business successfully, I want to discuss what to do when the lights go out, the landlord locks you out, the IRS attaches your bank, account or some other catastrophic event occurs. Do you fold up your tent and start looking for a new job? Or are there ways to salvage the business you have worked so hard to build and that is your most precious asset?

Fortunately, most situations look a lot worse than they are. I often receive frantic calls from clients who think their world has come to an end. Faced with IRS garnishment, lawsuits, foreclosures, repossessions, or attachments, they feel like their world is collapsing around them and that all hope has been lost. One such case was an owner of a cab company who called me, frantic, one afternoon after the constable had just carted off everything in her offices.

She had made a fundamental mistake in ignoring a lawsuit that had been filed against her. It's amazing how many SBO think that if they don't pick up their certified mail or ignore a citation served upon them, that nothing will happen to them. This head-in-the-sand mentality is a sure ticket to disaster, as my client found out when the constable showed up with two big trucks to haul away all her personal property.

Running a cab company with no radio equipment or telephones is rather difficult, so it was critical to get everything returned immediately. I only know of two ways to accomplish that: pay off the judgment that is being executed or file a Chapter 11. Since my client was essentially broke, Chapter 11 was the only thing that we could do. Several days later our client's property was returned and she was back in business.

The key to surviving any catastrophe is to keep calm and get professional help immediately. If it's a medical emergency, you call an ambulance or go to the emergency room. When you get served with a lawsuit you should immediately call an attorney so that the matter can be defended. Don't think you can be your own attorney. The law is very complicated and the procedure for prosecuting and defending lawsuits is very precise. An individual without legal training isn't going to be able to put up an effective defense. One of my clients found this out the hard way.

One evening I was just pulling into my garage when my cell phone rang. I answered the call and it was a frantic SBO who had just had his business put into a receivership. A receivership is where a third party, appointed by the court, is placed into control of a business for the benefit of creditors. This usually ends up in the liquidation of the business or a Chapter 7 bankruptcy. This SBO had been rather rudely put out of business.

When I asked him how it happened that he was put in receivership, he confessed that he had been sued and tried to defend the suit himself to save money. Unfortunately, the opposing counsel was a ruthless attorney who walked right over him in court and soon had control of his business. Receiverships are rather uncommon today, and had my client retained an attorney, he probably would have been able to successfully avoid the appointment of the receiver. Again, in this situation a Chapter 11 was the only way to stop the receivership and get this client back in control of his business.

When calamity strikes, the key to successfully dealing with it is to get an attorney immediately, identify your adversaries, weigh all the options available, and then pick an appropriate course of action.

Determining your adversaries is pretty easy as they are usually banging on the door. But sometimes adversaries aren't aggressive and may not have made any noise yet. It's important to do a complete analysis of all your creditors and contractual obligations to see what other potential claims there might be coming your way.

For instance, the immediate crisis may be an IRS garnishment of your bank account. Although this is annoying and will cost you whatever was in the bank account, it's not a devastating blow. But if a business owner can't pay his payroll taxes it's a good sign he's got other problems, too. The landlord may be about to lock him out or his vehicles may be in jeopardy of being repossessed.

Once you decide on a course of action, don't delay it's implementation. Time is always of the essence when it comes to defending yourself from attack. For instance, if you owe income taxes, the timing of filing your bankruptcy might be critical. Normally taxes are a priority debt but if they are more than three years old, they become an unsecured debt. It's always desirable to have taxes classified as unsecured because that means they don't have to be paid in full. Taxes, however, become secured if the government files a federal tax lien. Fortunately, the IRS usually isn't too quick to file these federal tax liens, but once they do file them, the taxpayer will likely have to pay the full taxes, plus penalty and interest. This happened in a recent case when a client came to see us about a Chapter 7 bankruptcy. His only creditor was the IRS, and most of the taxes were over three years old. Unfortunately, he had waited several months to deal with the problem. After we had all the papers together and were about to file the bankruptcy, he got a notice that a federal tax lien had been filed. With a lien filed, the bankruptcy wouldn't do him any good because the taxes were now secured by the equity in his homestead.

Another instance in which time is critical is with vehicles that are in danger of repossession. Often people wait until the repo man is stalking them before they contact us. A Chapter 13 usually solves this type of creditor problem, but it's important to file it before the vehicle is taken. Once the car is gone, there is danger that it can be sold and lost forever.

Normally a bank or finance company only has to give a borrower ten days notice of a private sale. If the sale takes place before the Chapter 13 is filed, the car may be lost. If the car is still in the possession of the bank or finance company when the bankruptcy is filed, then the car can't be sold without court permission. This usually affords the borrower the opportunity to get the car back but, if the creditor resists, another lawsuit or adversary proceeding, called a turnover, may have to be instituted. Of course, this involves time and money and may not be successful.

So the bottom line is that a small business owner should always react quickly to the first sign of trouble and deal with it quickly and effectively with professional help.

Chapter 13

Uncle Sam, the Sleeping Giant

Another common killer of small businesses is taxes. Instead of accepting the fact that taxes must be paid, small business owners invariably will try to figure out a way not to pay them or foign ignorance as to their obligation to pay them. There are many different types of taxes, most of which are complicated, and the tax reporting and compliance is extremely onerous.

What makes matters worse is that most government tax collectors are understaffed and often slow to do their job. They frequently let small business owners get hopelessly behind in their taxes before they come down on them. Many times clients have come to me when they owe fifty or a hundred thousand dollars in back payroll taxes. With penalties and interest accruing, there is no way they will ever be able to pay the taxes they owe. Often they have no understanding of how to handle payroll, calculate withholding, or making tax deposits. Consequently they have no idea they are getting themselves in deep trouble.

Property tax collectors are the worst. I've had clients come in who haven't paid property taxes in four or five years and nothing happens to them. Finally, when the taxing authority gets around to turning the matter over to an attorney, the amount due is so high the taxpayer can't come up with the money.

In Texas, the State Comptroller over the years has been the most aggressive tax collector. Frequently, I get calls from clients who have or are about to have their businesses shut down because they haven't filed their sales tax returns. Luckily the Comptroller hasn't let them get too far behind, so in most cases they quickly pay up. Once they realize they have to file the returns timely and pay the tax, they adjust to it and it has little impact on their business.

Because a small business owner can operate for years without paying property taxes or properly reporting and paying payroll taxes, the government ends up financing their businesses. Most of the time SBOs don't realize the business is losing money because they are not paying all their expenses. If they are on a cash basis for accounting purposes, which is common for small businesses, they may well feel like they are profitable when they are not.

Almost every Chapter 11 or 13 that I file for my small business clients involves substantial payroll tax liability issues. Tax liability has often been the primary reason a bankruptcy was necessary. For the SBO, collecting taxes for the federal government is a difficult, complicated, and hazardous task. It's a shame that a better system can't be found for handling this task. In the past, the government's response has been to increase the penalties and interest for not properly reporting and paying payroll taxes. This just makes matters worse, because when the small business owner finally realizes he must pay, the amount due is often double the actual amount of original tax liability and growing at a stunning rate. Even if the small business owner wanted to pay, he has no possible way of doing it short of bankruptcy.

In recent years Congress has changed the tax laws to require more frequent payroll deposits. This is a better approach, but one still difficult to enforce. Perhaps what needs to be done is to require a small business license which requires them to pass a test to show that they have a full understanding of how the tax system works and their responsibilities to pay and collect taxes for the government.

We require people to understand the driving laws before we let them out in the street, so why not make sure they understand the tax laws and other laws pertinent to operation of a small business?

A small business test would be a win-win solution because most SBOs want to be successful and want to pay all their bills. Rarely do I come across a business owner who is intentionally trying to evade taxes. Usually clients get into tax traps out of ignorance or because, when times get tough, they know the IRS will be the last one to come down on them. Optimistic by nature, the SBO believes in his heart that before the hammer will fall, his business will turn around and he'll be able to pay his taxes.

Of course the other solution is to take this liability off the shoulders of SBOs and eliminate the income tax altogether. But until that happens every SBO needs to learn how the tax systems works, accept the fact that these taxes must be paid, and then make it his first priority to properly report and pay his taxes. If this is too difficult, then the easy solution, and the one I use, is to hire a payroll service so you don't have to mess with it. These services are generally very cheap when you consider the burden they take off your shoulders, and they will allow you to focus on more important aspects of your small business.

Chapter 14

Dealing With An Angry Revenue Officer

Any SBO who has dealt with a revenue officer from the IRS collection branch knows it isn't a pleasant experience. More importantly, it's very dangerous because, from the moment the conversation begins, the agent's primary purpose is to get information from the taxpayer that will help in collecting the taxes. That's why a small business owner should never meet with the IRS alone. The first thing they should do when they get a notice, phone call, or visit from a revenue officer, is to call their accountant or attorney.

It's very easy for an unsuspecting taxpayer to give an agent incorrect or misleading information simply because of the pressure, anxiety, and anger the taxpayer may be feeling. The taxpayer is frequently so intimidated that the only thought on his mind is to give the agent what he wants and get rid of him. This can be disastrous, as agents often get evidence against you from material they never requested in the first place. Worse yet, they may find evidence pointing to problems in previous years.

If possible, the taxpayer should avoid the meeting entirely and let the tax professional handle it. After all, the owner's time is best spent in sales, marketing, and production, and they should avoid distractions when professionals can be hired to deal with them. An owner has enough pressure and stress just operating the business without having unpleasant confrontations with revenue officers.

Once your tax professional determines what tax liabilities you have, there are numerous ways to deal with it.

The most frequent is simple installment agreements. These can either be negotiated or unilateral agreements. A negotiated installment agreement is one that your tax professional works out with IRS for the payment taxes over a period of time, usually less than a year. For an agreed periodic payment, the IRS agrees to leave you alone. If you miss a payment or fail to fully comply with the tax laws in the future, the installment agreement will be terminated.

Many of my clients have suffered because of this rule. I can think of two clients who owed the IRS over a hundred thousand dollars and had somehow managed to get a revenue officer to agree to a $500 per month installment payout. This payment, of course, didn't even pay the interest on the amount due, but because the client convinced them that it was the best they could do, the revenue officer agreed to it.

Incredible as it may seem, both of these clients allowed their agreements to be terminated because they failed to timely file a subsequent tax return! Once the agreement was terminated, the IRS assigned new revenue agents who weren't nearly as generous as the former ones.

The first thing that is required in a negotiated installment agreement is the completion of a detailed financial questionnaire. You must disclose to the IRS your complete financial situation or they won't even talk to you. Once this has been done there are formulas that determine what amount of money you must pay each month. This amount will invariably be much higher than you had expected and often is a very unrealistic number.

If you can't reach an agreement or you don't want to disclose all your finances to IRS, I often recommend a unilateral agreement. The way this works is you determine how much you can pay each month and just start making those payments. If the period is six months or a year, often IRS won't take any enforcement action against you and you've avoided close IRS scrutiny. This doesn't always work, but many times it will, simply because the IRS can see by your regular monthly payment that you are trying. Because they are so understaffed and overworked, it just stands to reason that the taxpayer who is making an effort to pay his or her taxes won't be as high a priority as the one who is not.

If an installment payout is not feasible because of the amount of tax due or you're assigned an unsympathetic revenue officer, the next possibility is an Offer in Compromise. This is a formal proposal to the IRS to pay them less than what is due. One advantage of an Offer in Compromise is that once it is properly submitted all enforcement action stops. That means if your wages have been garnished, your bank account attached, or property is about to be auctioned off, it will all be halted while the Offer in Compromise is being considered.

This is particularly advantageous as it often takes the IRS six months to a year to consider the offer. If the offer is rejected, you can appeal it and get another six months reprieve from paying the tax. And the chances are better at the appellate level that the offer will be accepted as the revenue officers assigned there are more sophisticated and objective.

Unfortunately, there are serious disadvantages to an Offer In Compromise: the interest continues to accrue, you must agree to extend the statute of limitations while the offer is being considered, and any failure to file future returns or subsequent taxes can cause the revocation of the agreement. So, unless you are very confident an Offer In Compromise will provide you the time you need to pay the taxes or that it will be accepted, it's not a wise move.

So, how do you know whether IRS will accept an offer or not? That's not an easy question. Much depends on whose hands the offer ends up in. Some revenue officers are very rational and reasonable. Others are unsympathetic and arbitrary. I have found that an offer will likely be accepted if:

(1) it's unlikely the taxpayer will be able to pay the tax, (2) there is a question of whether the tax is really legitimate, or (3) the taxpayer offers to pay the tax over a period of time and obviously doesn't have the ability to pay it in a lump sum.

In the first instance, if the taxpayer is aged, permanently disabled, or incompetent the IRS will likely accept any reasonable Offer in Compromise because they know that it will be more than they would be likely to collect anyway.

Secondly, if the revenue officer considering the offer suspects the taxes weren't legitimate in the first place, he or she might agree to an offer that provides for the payment of the correct amount. A common example is when the taxpayer is assessed additional taxes based on erroneous information the IRS received from a third party, but fails to dispute it. If the revenue officer is provided proof that the information given them was wrong, he or she may agree to the offer even though it is too late to dispute the assessment.

This is one positive thing I've learned about the IRS. If you can convince them that the taxes shouldn't have been assessed in the first place, they will usually abate the tax even though legally it's too late to contest it. I don't think they have to do this, but I have found they usually will.

Finally, if the taxpayer acknowledges they owe the tax but just needs some time to pay it, usually an Offer In Compromise that provides for an installment payout of up to three years can be worked out. Whether interest continues to accrue during this time is negotiable. Sometimes even penalties can be knocked off as part of the agreement.

Although some tax practitioners advertise that they often are able to routinely negotiate payout of 25 to 33 cents on the dollar, I haven't been able to do that. Usually if a client is younger than 60, in good health, and employable, the IRS is not likely to accept an Offer In Compromise for less than what is owed. Perhaps the people advertising the ability to get large percentage reductions have connections in the IRS. I have found that former revenue officers or high officials in the IRS who retire into private practice often do have connections that give them an advantage over the rest of us. If you find someone like that, hire them and take advantage of their special relationship. I would ask for references though, to be sure they can really deliver the deal they say they can.

A final word about the IRS. Don't be intimidated by them. They are just another creditor. They have to abide by rules and regulations just like the rest of us. The key is to get professional help immediately and respond timely to whatever they throw at you. With the IRS, time is usually in your favor, so develop a long-term strategy to deal with your tax problem and stick with it.

Bankruptcy is often your best bet when it comes to dealing with a serious tax issue. Many taxes, such as income taxes, are dischargable if more than three years has elapsed since they were assessed. Even if the taxes are not dischargable, a Chapter 11 or 13 offers the ability to pay out whatever is owed over a period of three to six years. Chapter 13 even provides for the payment of the tax liability over a three-to five-year period without interest!

Whether a small business owner must file a Chapter 13 or 11 depends on several factors. If the business is a corporation, limited liability company, or partnership, a Chapter 11 would most likely be required. If the owner is operating as a sole proprietor, then a Chapter 13 would be appropriate unless his unsecured debt is over $250,000 or secured debt is over $1,000,000. In this case the sole proprietor would have to file Chapter 11.

What makes a bankruptcy attractive, beyond the ability to pay out the amount due, is the automatic stay. This is a court order which prohibits creditors, including the IRS and other taxing authorities, from taking any enforcement action against the person filing the bankruptcy, who is called "the debtor." This relief is extremely important in that it allows the SBO debtor to get all his creditors off his back so he can concentrate on repairing his troubled business.

The downside with bankruptcy, of course, is the damage it does to a business owner's credit. Many times, however, the credit has already been damaged if a tax lien has been filed, a car repossessed, or an account garnished. Whereas a bankruptcy may be on an SBO's record for up to ten years, some creditors will still give an SBO credit after the bankruptcy is over. As time goes on, more and more creditors will consider you for credit if you have a good job and haven't run up a lot of new debt. In fact, many bankruptcy clients are astounded when just several months after they file bankruptcy they start getting pre-approved credit card applications in the mail!

Bankruptcy doesn't carry the tremendous stigma that it did in years past. Several million people file bankruptcy each year, so many banks and financial institutions are tapping into this market. They are willing to take the risk of loaning to this segment of the population because the potential profits are so great. They will be restrictions of course, bigger down payments required, and higher interest rates, but at least there will be lenders out there willing to provide financing if it is really needed.

Chapter 15

State and Local Taxes

Whereas state and local taxes aren't likely to put a small business under, they can cause the SBO a lot of grief if they are overlooked or ignored. Fortunately, in Texas there is no state income tax. For SBOs in other states, reporting and paying state income taxes can be nearly as burdensome as federal payroll taxes. The key, again, is to accept the fact that these taxes have to be paid, and withhold and make deposits each pay period so there is little opportunity to inadvertently spend that money.

In Texas and many other states, the state imposes a franchise tax. This is a very annoying tax that SBOs often ignore. The problem with ignoring this tax for a corporation or limited liability company is the fact that your corporate charter will eventually be revoked. This can be devastating if a SBO gets in trouble and needs to rely on the liability protection that a corporation or limited liability company will provide. Suddenly an SBO may find himself personally liable for all the company debts simply because he didn't file this return and pay the tax.

Another problem is that the company will not be allowed to prosecute or defend itself in court if these taxes are not paid and the charter is allowed to be forfeited. This can be remedied simply by filing the return and paying the tax, but many SBOs don't know this and let creditors take default judgments against them at will. Fortunately, the Texas legislature recently enacted a $150,000 income exclusion for small businesses that will eliminate the franchise tax problem for smaller SBOs. But for those outside Texas or with revenues over $150,000 the franchise may still be a problem.

Personal and real property taxes are almost always a line item in the bankruptcies I file. Since few taxing authorities vigorously prosecute those who don't pay them, they tend to be a low priority. Over time they can become quite large and difficult to pay. The best way to handle them is to establish an escrow fund. This can be done with the mortgage company or by creation of an escrow fund at a bank or savings and loan. Then each month you deposit one twelfth of the amount you will need for the year. This can also be done with insurance so that when the time comes to make the payment the money is in hand. Don't think you can pull these large payments from current cash flow. It just won't happen and you will just end up paying late fees and penalties.

I have had one unlucky SBO in Chapter 13 for ten years simply because she didn't have the discipline to pay her property taxes. She was a self employed cleaning woman and barely made enough to survive. She owned her house outright so the taxes were not escrowed each month. When she was unable to pay the taxes for three years, the City of Dallas turned her over to an attorney and a suit was filed. She didn't hire an attorney to contest the suit, so before long the property was put up for sale at a tax auction. Without enough money to pay rent, if she had lost her house she may have ended up on the street. That's when she sought our help.

We put her in Chapter 13 and were able to stop the sale of her home. The problem was that she now had to make monthly payments to the bankruptcy trustee. This didn't leave enough money left over for her to escrow taxes for the following year, so she was always getting behind on her payments. When she got too far behind, she'd get dismissed and we'd have to start over again. Unfortunately, repetitive bankruptcy filing is considered an abuse of the bankruptcy system, so two or three bankruptcy filings is the most anyone can hope to file. If our client lets this bankruptcy get dismissed, she will may end up homeless.

Sales and use taxes aren't as much of a problem for the SBO because a sales tax permit and a bond are usually required before a business can open. To get the permit, SBOs are given instructions as to what is expected of them. The SBO must remit the taxes periodically and, if they don't the taxing authorities come down on them quickly and effectively.

There are a myriad of other taxes and assessments state and local governments assess against the SBO's property. Assessments for street improvements is one that can be quite devastating to SBO. When you buy real property, be sure and find out if the state, county, or city plans to widen the road in front of your property. These assessments can be very large and jeopardize the unsuspecting SBO's ownership of the property should he be unable to pay it.

Finally, I have had many SBOs devastated when they purchase or lease property and find out that, in order to get an occupancy permit they must make thousands of dollars of repairs. I know of several instances in which businesses that were planning to make a quick move to improve business or get a better lease rate, ended up out of business for several months while required repairs or upgrades were completed. Compliance with the American Disabilities Act, environmental laws and local codes and ordinances are usually the sources of these types of costly delays and business interruptions. If you have a realtor he or she should check out all of this for you. If you don't use a realtor, you will have to do it yourself or hire an attorney to do it for you. But, whatever you do, don't ignore these most serious problems.

Chapter 16

When The Constable Knocks

When the constable knocks on the door, the natural inclination is to escape out the back door. SBOs seem to think that if they ignore a problem it will go away. This is not at all true. Problems need to be quickly identified and strategies developed to deal with them. When the constable comes by, invite him in and offer him a cup of coffee. After all, he is just the messenger and has no animosity towards you. You need to treat him nicely because if he ever comes by to execute on a judgment, you may need him to cut you some slack.

Lawsuits are usually long-term problems. They generally drag on for months or years. They're normally not an immediate threat to you if you hire an attorney immediately and answer the lawsuit. So take the citation and call your attorney immediately. In Texas you have about three weeks to answer a lawsuit (the first Monday that comes after 20 days from date of service). This doesn't mean you have to actually go to court on this date, but simply that an answer must be filed before that date arrives.

If you don't file an answer, then a default judgment will be taken against you and, essentially the plaintiff will automatically get whatever relief he has asked for. *Don't ever let this happen, get and attorney and answer the lawsuit.* If you can't afford an attorney, you can answer the suit yourself, but the answer must be in writing and delivered to the court clerk. For a few bucks, the attorney you can't afford to have represent you might show you how to answer the suit Pro Se. Answering Pro Se is what it is called when an individual answers a lawsuit without an attorney. An individual always has the right to answer a lawsuit himself. If you are a corporation or partnership, you might have to get an attorney to answer. It is best to check with the individual court, as different courts have different rules.

If all else fails, go to the library or a bookstore and you can usually find a form book with the proper format for filing an answer. It's actually very simple. But get the lawsuit answered. Some people think just because the facts in the suit are a pack of lies that they don't have to worry about the lawsuit. This is not true. Those pack of lies will be considered the truth by the court if you don't answer the lawsuit!

After the lawsuit is answered, you will have some time to breathe. Litigation is a slow process, so use this breathing spell to find an attorney you can afford. Nobody likes to pay attorneys but sometimes you have to bite the bullet and get one. If you absolutely can't afford an attorney, call the local bar association and get a list of legal service agencies that provide services to the poor. If you are in business for yourself, this might be difficult as free legal services are designed for those without a job or any means of support.

Once the suit has been answered and you have an attorney articulating your position, you can relax. The vast majority of lawsuits settle and never go to court. This will probably happen in your case. Litigation is expensive and most plaintiffs don't want to bear the expense of litigating through trial. Settle your case and get it over with. It's better to pay out a little so you can refocus on operating your business.

If the lawsuit is one that can't be settled and threatens your ability to do business, then you may have to consider Chapter 13 or 11 to stay in business. Don't give up. There are almost always ways to get out of trouble. You just need to weigh your options with a good attorney and come up with a viable game plan. Many successful business owners have only achieved their success after failing more than once at making a business work. Often only experiencing defeat can make you wise enough and strong enough to be successful.

There are a few types of lawsuits that will require your immediate attention and response: garnishments, injunctions, attachments, and executions. These are extraordinary legal maneuvers which can immediately threaten your ability to operate your business. An attorney must be immediately retained because these actions are highly complex, and an individual without legal training couldn't possibly deal with them effectively

A garnishment is the legal process where a creditor seizes one of your assets being held by a third party like a bank. The IRS uses this tactic a lot to take money from your bank account. This can be very disruptive because you usually don't know about the garnishment until after it has happened. By this time, checks are bouncing and your business is in serious jeopardy. Garnishments can also be used to freeze assets that belong to you but others have in their possession. For instance, if a customer owes you money, your creditor could garnish that money, forcing your customer to pay that money to them rather than to you.

Injunctions also require your immediate attention and response because they are court orders prohibiting you from taking certain actions or requiring you to do something. They initially start out as temporary restraining orders (TROs), then may mature into a temporary injunction, and finally they may become a permanent injunction. If you don't pay attention to this type of court order, you can be found in contempt and fined or thrown in jail. The most common TROs that you will likely run into involve divorce actions. If a spouse of an SBO decides to file divorce she will likely get a TRO that prohibits the SBO from doing anything out of the ordinary course of business. If this happens, you need to consult an attorney immediately to be sure you don't violate the TRO.

TROs can also be used in conjunction with other lawsuits such as partnership dissolution. I have had several cases in which partners are disgruntled and want to prohibit other partners from using partnership money or from taking certain action. The courts will often issue a TRO to preserve the status quo and prevent any one partner from taking advantage of the other partners in breach of the partnership business.

Attachments and executions usually occur when a creditor gets a judgment against you. Once property of an SBO is attached, control over that asset is gone. If you don't get an attorney's assistance immediately, you may lose that asset. If the attachment or execution is the result of a default judgment taken against you, you may be able to stop it by filing a motion for a new trial or putting up a bond while you appeal the judgment.

What you can't afford to do is sit around moaning and groaning about how you've been victimized by the legal system. You have to get an attorney and fight for your rights. If you don't, your creditors will win and you will be out of business. If you thought being a SBO was going to be easy, well now you know that preconception was wrong. If you don't want to fight, then go to work for someone else.

Assuming you are in a normal lawsuit, once you have filed an answer, the discovery period commences. This is basically a time when each party can require the other to provide information that might help your case. This exchange of information is done by requests for disclosure, interrogatories, requests for admissions, deposition, and requests for production.

In Texas we have a pleading called "request for disclosure" which requires each party to disclose to each other certain basic information such as: the correct identity of the parties, who the witnesses are, what legal theories they plan to invoke, and if they have obtained any witness statements. This is information that parties almost always need, so the law requires they provide this information automatically if the other side requests it.

Interrogatories are used to obtain additional information not provided in the request for disclosure. Each side can ask each other questions which must be answered in writing under oath within 30 days. This is useful in getting specific information such as the identity and location of documents, dates, explanation of events, and background information on the parties.

Requests for production allow each party to require the other to let them look at all the records that might relate to the case. This is often critical to determine the facts necessary to prove a case. These documents must be produced and made available for copying by the other side so that each party will have time to analyze the documents and use them at the time of trial.

Depositions of parties and witnesses can be taken. This is a formal face to face confrontation in front of a court reporter, attorneys, and the parties involved. The witnesses appear by agreement or under subpoena. Witnesses can be made to bring documents by attaching a subpoena *duces tecum* specifying the items desired.

Finally, each side can send requests for admissions which are questions the opponent must either admit or deny. They are designed to save time at trial by determining uncontested issues in advance so the focus at the time of trial can be on the contested issues.

Once the discovery is complete, the court will usually order mediation. This is a great time to settle your case and avoid a costly trial. The mediation usually takes place at a neutral site and begins with an opening session. The purpose of the opening session is to allow the mediator to explain the process, have each attorney summarize their case, and then let the parties explain their positions.

This is your opportunity to tell your opponent what you think about their case. It's a good time to vent and let our your frustration and anger so that meaningful negotiations can take place.

After the opening session, each party goes off to a separate room and the mediator shuffles back and forth taking offers of settlement between the parties. During this time the mediator points out strengths and weaknesses of each parties' case and, hopefully, a settlement is finally reached.

It's important that you have an open mind at mediation and negotiate in good faith. Remember anything can happen at trial. No matter how good your case is, you could lose at trial and suffer a devastating blow to your small business. It's always better to stay out of the courthouse if at all possible and avoid total defeat. Remember you are a business owner and should be driven by the bottom line, not emotions and pride.

If you don't settle and do end up in the courthouse, don't be surprised when your attorney wants a large retainer before the trial begins. The reason for this is that if you lose, your legal bill for the trial will be the last thing you ever want to pay. Remember your attorney is in business too, so he has to consider his bottom line just like you do.

Chapter 17

Bankruptcy: Friend or Foe?

For the SBO, a customer's bankruptcy can be devastating. Rarely is there a reserve for the loss of a large receivable. Even if it is a Chapter 11 or 13, which provides for the payment of a portion of the debt, it often takes months or years to actually receive any part of it. All the SBO can do is file a proof of claim and wait. Occasionally there are objections that can be filed and a bankruptcy attorney should always be consulted to see if there is any way to get the claim bumped up to secured or priority status. In some cases, it may be that the claim is non-dischargable. So don't give up. See a bankruptcy attorney and explore your options.

In many cases, the SBO will have to file bankruptcy himself for his own protection. If he wants to stay in business, it will be a Chapter 11 or 13. If he wants to shut down the business or if he is in the service business and has no business assets, a Chapter 7 might be appropriate.

Chapter 7 is designed to clean the slate and give the person filing a fresh start. To be eligible for bankruptcy, the SBO must prove (1) he has more liabilities than assets, or (2) that he is unable to pay his debts as they become due.

If an SBO qualifies for Chapter 7, he must surrender all his non-exempt property to the trustee appointed in the case. He is allowed to keep his exempt property such as automobiles, household furnishings, personal effects, qualified employee benefit accounts, life insurance policies, tools of the trade, and homestead. He must choose between the state and federal exemptions which have significantly different provisions concerning what property can be kept. In Texas and Florida, the state exemptions are more favorable but, in certain cases, the federal exemptions may be appropriate. The attorney will help the SBO decide the appropriate exemption election.

Getting a discharge is the main objective of a bankruptcy, as it is the release and forgiveness of certain debts. After the discharge creditors are prohibited from attempting to collect the discharged debts.

A secured creditor is the one who holds a mortgage or lien on property owned by the SBO. Secured claims only extend to the actual value of the collateral and the remainder of the debt is unsecured. Secured debts may be reaffirmed if the SBO wants to keep the collateral, or surrendered if he does not. A reaffirmation is a new promise to pay a debt that would otherwise be discharged. Reaffirmations must be made before the discharge, must be in writing, and may be revoked prior to discharge or within 60 days after it is made. An SBO debtor has no obligation to reaffirm a debt.

A Chapter 13, sometimes called a "debtor adjustment," is designed to allow the SBO debtor to reorganize his personal or business affairs. The objective is to allow the SBO debtor to keep certain assets in exchange for paying a portion of the debt that otherwise could have been discharged in Chapter 7. These payments are made to a trustee and extend over a period of three to five years. For the SBO debtor in trouble, a Chapter 13 may provide a way to save the business.

To be eligible for Chapter 13 the SBO must be an individual, have a regular income, have secured debt of $750,000 or less, and unsecured debt of $250,000 or less. In Chapter 13, a plan is submitted for approval, called confirmation, which will provide for a monthly payment to be made to the standing chapter 13 trustee. The chapter 13 trustee distributes the plan payments to the creditors as set forth in the chapter 13 plan and in accordance with the requirements of the bankruptcy code.

The amount of an SBO's plan payment will depend on his income and allowable expenses. He will have to prepare a reasonable expense budget that will be subtracted from his income to arrive at the amount available for plan payments. The amount must be paid for a minimum of three years and maximum of five years.

The Chapter 13 discharge is much more extensive than in Chapter 7. Fewer objections are allowed, and some debts which are not dischargable in Chapter 7 are discharged in chapter 13. Most debts not paid through the Chapter 13 plan will be discharged upon the completion of the plan. Secured debts will still have to be paid if the SBO debtor desires to keep the collateral.

If the SBO debtor's circumstances change during the course of the Chapter 13 case, they may be eligible to modify their plan to take these changes into consideration. For example, if one spouse loses a job, the plan may have to be modified to reduce the payments or suspend payments until the spouse gets a new job.

The SBO debtor receives immediate relief from creditors the moment a bankruptcy is filed, as an automatic stay or court order takes effect that prohibits creditors from making contact with an SBO debtor or attempting to collect their debt.

To commence the bankruptcy process the SBO debtor must complete schedules and a statement of financial affairs. The SBO debtor will need to provide to his attorney the name and address of all his creditors and the balance owed to each, complete asset information, and copies of his last three income tax returns. He will also be asked to prepare a budget of the SBO debtor's monthly income and expenses.

Several weeks after the bankruptcy is filed, the SBO debtor will have to attend a creditor meeting before the trustee appointed in the case so he can determine if your paperwork is in order. At this time creditors can attend and ask you questions. The SBO debtor and his spouse, if married, must attend this meeting for the bankruptcy to be finalized.

There is a downside to filing any kind of bankruptcy that the SBO debtor must be aware of prior to filing. The most significant is the effect bankruptcy will have on his credit. A credit bureau can show a Chapter 13 on a credit report for seven years and a Chapter 7 for up to ten years from the date of filing. If the SBO debtor's credit is already damaged, this might not matter. Or, if there is no other option, the loss of credit might be an acceptable risk.

Another drawback that SBOs don't always understand is that in Chapter 7 they must surrender any non-exempt property such as investments, non-exempt real estate, and cash immediately after filing. In Chapter 13 they may be allowed to keep non-exempt property but they will have to pay additional monies into the plan equal to the value of the non-exempt property that they keep. The theory is that unsecured creditors should recover more from a Chapter 13 than a Chapter 7.

The trustee can make an SBO debtor turn over assets acquired after the filing too, such as tax refunds, inheritances, insurance proceeds, lottery winnings, and other windfalls. The SBO debtor must report any such receipts to the Chapter 7 trustee promptly so the trustee can decide whether to claim those assets or not. Large sums will always be taken, but many times smaller amounts will be abandoned by the trustee. In Chapter 13 the SBO debtor must amend his schedules and Chapter 13 plan to reflect the receipt of any subsequent receipts or windfalls.

Another risk in filing bankruptcy is the adverse publicity that often results. This is particularly bad for the SBO debtor trying to reorganize a business. Sometimes sales will decline as some customers are scared off by the bankruptcy.

Creditors who owe the SBO debtor money will suddenly get the idea they don't have to pay their debt because the business is in bankruptcy. This is a false, but common belief. The SBO debtor will have to stay on top of his accounts receivable and advise anyone owing money that their obligation must be paid in a timely manner or it will be turned over to an attorney.

There are some debts that Chapter 7 will not discharge such as certain taxes, student loans, child support, alimony, intentional injuries to persons and property, and liability as a result of driving while intoxicated. If an SBO debtor has any of these types of debts on the date of filing, he will have to arrange for payment of these debts outside the bankruptcy.

Secured debt, of course, is not discharged by a Chapter 7 or 13 bankruptcy, so the SBO debtor will have to continue to pay such secured debts or surrender the collateral. If the collateral is surrendered, any deficiency will be discharged. Many times assets previously purchased are no longer needed in the business. Bankruptcy provides the option to surrender those assets to the creditor and get relief from that obligation. A similar provision applies to leases and contracts. This ability to pick and choose assets and debts to reaffirm is a critical tool for the SBO debtor which often is the key to a successful reorganization.

Chapter 11 is another type of reorganization for individuals with larger estates, corporations, partnerships, and limited liability companies. It is dramatically different than Chapter 13 in cost, procedure, and complexity. Whereas a Chapter 13 may only cost the SBO $2,000 or $3,000, a Chapter 11 will be at least $10,000 to $20,000. A Chapter 13 is administered by the standing Chapter 13 trustee who takes care of much of the work that ordinarily would have to be done by the attorney. In a Chapter 11 the attorney has to do everything. Consequently, there will many more meetings with the attorney, hearings before the court, and administrative red tape in order to prosecute a case from start to finish.

Other differences include a much higher filing fee, the possible appointment of an unsecured creditors' committee, closer financial scrutiny, and the filing of a detailed disclosure document similar to what would be required in a stock offering. An accountant is almost always needed to help prove the feasibility of the plan by making future projections of how the plan will perform financially.

One advantage to a Chapter 11 is that it has more flexibility. The term is not limited to five years as is the case in the Chapter 13, and the attorney can be much more creative in the specifics of the plan. Unlike a Chapter 13, the Chapter 11 plan will be put to a vote, so there is some politics involved.

There are some basic requirements for filing either a Chapter 11 or 13. Any debts owed at the time of filing must be listed on the debtor's schedules and cannot be paid during the plan without a court order. Debts and expenses incurred during Chapter 13 or 11 must be kept current. The SBO debtor is not allowed to get further in debt without permission of the court.

What this means is that the debtor must be able to operate at a profit immediately after filing bankruptcy. This is the downfall of most debtors. When they first file they don't always know what has gone wrong, so they don't know what adjustments need to be made to be profitable. So, oftentimes, in months two or three of the bankruptcy, they will be already starting to get behind. In a Chapter 11 the U.S. Trustee's office monitors each debtor-in-possession carefully and, if they get behind on post-petition payments, the trustee assigned to the case is likely to file a motion to dismiss the case or convert it to Chapter 7.

Consequently, it's extremely important at the very outset of a Chapter 13 or 11 to identify what has caused the SBO to be in the predicament he finds himself and take swift, effective measures to resolve that issue. If the problem can't realistically be fixed, then a Chapter 7 should be filed and the business shut down. There's no point in prolonging the agony if the business can't be saved.

Bankruptcy is a very useful and powerful tool for the SBO in trouble. Obviously, it should only be used if there is no other way out, but once it is invoked, it will likely be the best chance the SBO has for survival.

Chapter 18

Loan Consolidations & Workouts

Sometimes bankruptcy will not be a viable option for the SBO for a number of reasons. A typical situation might be that the debtor has paid off a debt to a family member. If he files bankruptcy, the money that went to the family member might have to be returned to the debtor's estate as a preference. Let's say two brothers, Luke and Wally, are contractors. Luke is good with money and has accumulated a nice estate. Wally, on the other hand, spends everything he has and is always broke. Consequently, Wally is always borrowing from Luke. Despite Luke's help, Wally can't make ends meet and finally gets so far behind that bankruptcy seems like his only option.

The problem is: he had previously borrowed $140,000 from Luke and over the last year has paid him back $75,000 leaving a balance of $65,000. If he files bankruptcy, Luke loses $65,000, which he is prepared to write off because he loves his brother. But then his bankruptcy attorney tells him that not only will he lose $65,000, but he'll have to pay the bankruptcy trustee back the $75,000 that he received during the previous year.

Preference law is one of the most difficult legal principles to explain to SBOs. What the law tries to accomplish is to put all creditors on an equal footing. Since family members have inside information and influence, it is common for them to be paid all, or at least some, of what is owed to them before the bankruptcy is filed. This would be unfair to general creditors, so the law states that anything received by an insider (family member, employee, partner, etc.) must be returned to the bankruptcy trustee to be distributed to general creditors in accordance with the priority system of the bankruptcy code.

A preference can also occur between unrelated creditors of the bankrupt debtor. The time is shortened from one year to 90 days, however. I recall one case in which a manufacturers' representative for a clothing manufacturer, Brandon, was owed commissions of about $60,000. This was the only company he represented, so he was very upset to learn his manufacturer was having financial difficulties. When he pressed the company for payment of his commissions, they put him off, but eventually gave him a check for $35,000, claiming there were some issues with the balance due. Several weeks later the company filed bankruptcy.

Brandon was upset to have lost $25,000 but glad to get some money at least to tide him over until he found a new company to represent. Then one day he got a letter demanding that he return the $35,000 that had been paid him because it had been paid within 90 days of filing bankruptcy. Flabbergasted, he shot back a nasty letter to the bankruptcy trustee telling him that it was his money and he was keeping it.

It wasn't long after that he was served with a citation advising him that an adversary proceeding had been filed against him in a bankruptcy court in Maryland. At this point he conferred with a bankruptcy attorney and found out he may, in fact, have to return the money.

So, if an SBO has paid a preference to someone and he doesn't want them to have to return the money, bankruptcy will not be an option until the preference period has gone by. Another reason he might not want to file is that he has personally guaranteed so much of the debt that filing a bankruptcy will not really be of much help. Just as soon as the corporation files Chapter 11, the creditors will start coming straight to him, so if he files bankruptcy for the company he will have to file personal bankruptcy as well.

In this case, the SBO may want to borrow money for a workout or a bill consolidation loan. A workout is the payment of a debt over an extended period of time or satisfaction of the debt for less than 100% of the balance due. For instance, I often can settle old credit card debts for 50 cents on the dollar. So, if an SBO who owes $30,000 in credit card debt gives me $15,000, I can usually convince the credit card companies to accept this amount in full satisfaction of their debts. This is just one of many types of workouts that can be negotiated with creditors. The key is to convince the creditor of the dire circumstances of the SBO and the tremendous risk he has of never getting paid. Usually a creditor would rather take a sure thing now rather than speculate on an uncertain future.

A bill consolidation loan is a new loan obtained for the purpose of paying off several existing debts with the net result usually being a longer payout at a lower interest rate. In this case if the SBO has $30,000 in credit card debt at 21% interest and is paying the 2% minimum monthly payment of $600. If he only pays the minimum payment each month he may never get the loan paid off. So he goes and gets a loan for $30,000 at 10% interest payable in 15 years. His monthly payment is now only $322 which improves his cash flow dramatically.

Whether the SBO can get a loan for either of these purposes will depend on several factors whether or not: (1) his credit is still good enough, (2) he has collateral for a loan, or (3) he can get a co-signer. One common source of funds for a workout is home equity. Lenders love it because they can have a fully secured loan and, if the debtor defaults, there is usually enough equity in the property to be assured of a full recovery.

Another common way to get loan consolidation or workout funding is with a loan guaranteed by someone with good credit or someone who has collateral to pledge. Friends, family members, or partners are usually good sources for this type of help. In one case a contractor, Peter Walker, was very popular and always busy. Unfortunately, he didn't know how to run his construction business and got farther and farther behind on his payroll taxes, until the IRS was about ready to shut him down. Since payroll taxes are not dischargable in bankruptcy, a workout was his best option.

In this case Peter teamed up with a friend, Tom Banks, who knew how to run a business but knew nothing about building a house. Tom loaned him the money to pay the IRS with the promise that they would do future business together: Tom running the new venture and Peter handling operations. Thus bankruptcy was avoided and a new enterprise was begun that probably had a much better chance of survival than Peter had as a sole proprietor.

Another alternative to bankruptcy is the workout. What this involves is negotiating with creditors to get them to take less than what is owed to them. For instance, if $100,000 is due to creditors, the debtor might propose a workout of $25,000, or 25 cents on the dollar. Whether or not creditors will accept a workout depends on whether they can be convinced that it is a good deal. For instance, I often tell creditors that they can either accept 25% now or chance getting zero if a bankruptcy is filed. Some will tell me to take a hike, but most will reluctantly accept the lesser amount because, as a practical matter, it is very difficult to collect from a creditor in trouble. This is particularly true if the debtor is out of state.

Sometimes workouts take months or years to accomplish, as some creditors will resist the workout and file suit to collect the entire amount. Others will simply just stubbornly refuse to agree. Over time most will succumb and accept the amount offered. The ones who hold out will either end up getting paid in full or getting nothing.

In one instance I contacted a creditor of a florist I was doing a workout for and offered $18,000, which was 50% of what was owed. The creditor was very hostile and told me his attorney would be calling me back. The attorney was equally belligerent and asked if I would accept service for my client. Over the next nine months while we were litigating this case, all the funds we had for the workout were exhausted. Eventually, the hostile creditor got tired of the expense and hassle of litigation and offered to take the $18,000. We politely informed him that there were no longer any funds available for settlement.

In another case the opposite happened. The creditor jumped right in and filed suit. He prosecuted the suit vigorously and would have jeopardized the entire workout had we not settled with him. In this case he finally accepted an 80% payout, which was much higher than anyone else received, but necessary under the circumstances.

My standard advice to clients is, if possible, stay out of court. Once you surrender yourself to the jurisdiction of the courts, then you have lost control over your life and must accept whatever judgment the court imposes. So, if it isn't absolutely necessary to file a bankruptcy, then a workout is the best way to go. Often you can accomplish nearly as much on your own without giving a judge control over your destiny.

Chapter 19

Employees — Double Trouble

Good employees are critical to the success of any small business. The owner usually can't do everything himself, although some owners try. It's important to find employees who are capable, dependable, and have a good, positive attitude. But often that is a very long and time-consuming process, which few employers have the time or patience to perform consistently. Consequently, the process is often short-circuited, resulting in substandard employees and performance.

In my own situation, finding good employees has been one of my most difficult tasks. Good legal secretaries and paralegals command high salaries. In my early years of practice, I couldn't afford an experienced paralegal or even a top notch legal secretary. As a result I had to hire inexperienced secretaries and train them. This wasn't a very efficient way to operate, as I was forced to spend my valuable time training employees.

To make matters worse, after I got a secretary or paralegal trained, she often would get lured away by a big firm who could pay her a much larger salary. This is just one of many problems in dealing with employees. Another big one is finding competent employees.

Prospective employees tend to exaggerate their experience and training. Few small business owners have the time or patience to thoroughly test employees to verify their skill level. Nor do they bother to verify resumes. It's human nature to trust people and to believe what they tell you.

Unfortunately, in today's world, this is a very perilous practice.

The process of screening and selecting employees can be delegated to professionals or employees trained specifically to perform that task. However, this can be very expensive, and there is no guarantee that the employee placed with your company will be any better than someone you personally hand picked.

Once you select and hire an employee, you then face a whole host of other issues such as payroll, health insurance, sick time, vacation pay, workman's compensation, and retirement. All of these are highly complex issues which few SBOs enjoy dealing with, yet failing to effectively deal with any one of them could be fatal to a small business.

For an SBO many of these issues can be handled by others. A payroll service can be employed to handle payroll, and a good insurance agent will do the paperwork for all your insurance needs. An actuary or brokerage house can handle your pension or 401K needs. It's important that the SBO is not distracted by these types of problems. Delegate them to other employees and professionals who are trained to handle them. Just be careful in the selection process. Get a referral from someone who has used them in the past and is very satisfied with their performance. Beware of second-hand and "brother-in-law" referrals, in which the person giving the referral has no personal knowledge of the professional's competence.

PART 3

TURNING IT AROUND

Chapter 20

Getting An Attorney

Once the business is stabilized, then all attention must be turned to making it profitable. Whatever mistakes have been made in the past must be identified and eliminated. To do this, an attorney, accountant, and possibly a business consultant will be needed. Think of your small business as a small kingdom at war. You are surrounded by armies ready to attack at any moment. They have one objective, and that is to take everything you own at any cost. Your attorney is the commander of your army—the army who will defend you while you're trying to rebuild your kingdom which holds all your worldly possessions. Pick your commander carefully, as his or her skill will be critical to your survival—and for godsakes, pay him so he won't abandon you.

It amazes me how SBOs in desperate trouble treat their attorneys. Often their bills are neglected or ignored altogether when they are in the heat of battle. The SBO often treats the attorney like he is just another creditor, expecting him to work without being paid. But few attorneys will put up with this and, if you run up a big bill with your attorney, you'll soon find yourself with a new, more dangerous creditor at your heels demanding payment. So remember, if you don't pay your army, they will neglect or abandon you, and always at a time when you can least afford to be defenseless.

If your attorney is so critical to your survival, how do you find the best one for the job? Usually, the best way is by referral. But only accept a referral from someone who has used the referred attorney in a similar situation. Many people refer an attorney they know nothing about. They may have seen him on TV, heard his ad on the radio, or found out about him from a friend or relative. Every week I get similar referrals of clients from people who don't know me. While I appreciate these referrals, you're not doing anyone a favor if you refer them to someone you know nothing about.

It is also important that the referred attorney is experienced in the area for which you are seeking representation. A friend might refer you an attorney who did a great job handling his divorce, but that same attorney is not likely to be the best person to guide you through a successful reorganization of your small business.

If you can't get a referral from someone who has successfully reorganized their business, then you may have to turn to a referral service. The local bar association is probably the best, but you still must be selective. The bar associations do not screen the attorneys who they recommend. Usually the criteria is simply that they are licensed to practice law, are a member of their association, and have malpractice insurance. You need to interview the attorney referred to you to be sure he or she is experienced in helping a small business under siege. The sure test of the attorney's ability is to ask the attorney for references from three small business owners who he has successfully reorganized. If he can't or won't provide those references, keep looking.

Once you have found the right attorney, confess to him all your sins. Be honest and tell him everything that might impact the defense of your business. Everything you tell your attorney is confidential, so don't be timid, shy, or too embarrassed to tell all. The worst thing for an attorney is to be blind-sided at trial or in a hearing. On one occasion I was helping a middle-aged woman shut down her failed business. It appeared to be a simple Chapter 7 bankruptcy, but she seemed to be a little more nervous than expected. I quizzed her about it and she said it was just her nature. At the creditors' meeting, her nervousness increased, and during my questioning she suddenly confessed to having $25,000 in cash stuffed under her mattress.

Of course, I was flabbergasted and greatly disturbed, because failing to disclose assets in a bankruptcy is a criminal offense. Fortunately, I was able to convince the trustee that the woman simply thought because the money wasn't in her checking account, she didn't have to report it. This is a common misconception of debtors. They think that by giving cash or property away to a friend or relative, they don't have to report it on their bankruptcy. My client was lucky she didn't end up in jail.

The sad thing is she lost $25,000, that she probably could have kept had she been honest with me. If I had known she had $25,000 we probably could have figured out how to legally keep it or spend it prior to filing bankruptcy. Since she wasn't honest with me, she lost the money and nearly ended up in jail.

Many states have so-called board certified attorneys, who have special training in a particular area of law practice. Whereas a board certified bankruptcy attorney may be excellent at getting you through bankruptcy, he may know nothing about the proper structure of your business, minimizing estate taxes, or handling employee issues. A general practitioner, who is a small businessman himself, may actually be better than the bankruptcy specialist.

Sometimes you will need more than one attorney to get you through the problems you face. In one instance we were representing a client who was having financial difficulties due to of an automobile accident. He had been cut off by a large truck and suffered a severe concussion that left him with brain damage. He could still function, but lost the ability to run his business. In this case, we were able to handle his personal injury claim and file a Chapter 13 bankruptcy to try to preserve his business until he could recover, but we were not competent to handle a Social Security disability claim. We, therefore, referred him to an attorney who specialized in Social Security disability and monitored that case closely while we prosecuted the other actions. If you need more than one attorney, hire them, but select just one to be in charge of all the others so he can coordinate your legal affairs during this critical reorganization period.

Once you have one or more attorneys, keep in touch with them. Be sure you advise them immediately of any communications from creditors or new circumstances that could impact your reorganization. Your attorneys should promptly return telephone calls, but if they don't, be persistent and don't give up until you have reached them. Attorneys are busy and often take too long to return phone calls. If you can't get through immediately to the attorney, talk to his secretary or legal assistant. They are usually much easier to contact and will have direct access to the attorney.

If communication with an attorney becomes too difficult or impossible, then hire a new one. You have the right to hire and fire your attorney at will, so don't be afraid to do so if necessary. This may be your one chance to get your business on track, so don't let a bad choice of an attorney keep you from attaining your goal. Remember it is your future that is at stake, so take charge of the situation and do what it takes to be successful.

Chapter 21

Form of Business

One of the first decisions that will have to be made during the reorganization process is what type of entity will best suit your business. Most small businesses come to me as sole proprietorships. This rarely is the optimal form of a business as it is important to keep the individual and business separated for efficiency and protection of personal assets. Usually a limited liability company, corporation, or limited partnership is what is needed.

A corporation has traditionally been the vehicle of choice for small businesses. It is a distinct entity, which is itself a taxpayer. It provides centralized management, liability protection to its stockholders, and free transferability of interests. It is well understood and recognized as the "normal" way to do business in America.

A limited liability company is a more recent breed of business entity, but it is rapidly becoming the obvious choice for the SBO. It provides the same centralized management, free transferability of interest, and liability protection, but has the option of being taxed itself or being taxed like a partnership. Normally, the SBO will elect to be taxed like a partnership so the profit and loss of the business will pass through to the owner directly. This eliminates any possibility of having profits taxed as a dividend and allows the SBO to use business losses to offset other personal income.

Occasionally a limited partnership will be the vehicle of choice if there are investors who want to put money in the business, but do not want operational responsibility. Limited partnerships can often provide tax advantages and other advantages that a corporation or limited liability company cannot. Therefore it is important to look closely at the business with your accountant and attorney and determine which type of organization is best.

Once the choice has been made a conversion must take place. This can be a fairly complicated process that must be done very carefully to avoid adverse tax consequences. If a conversion is not possible, sometimes the best approach is to shut down the old business and start over in a new business vehicle. Either way, it is important to get this done quickly, as the business vehicle in which you operate is the foundation upon which you will build your newly restructured business, and you want it to be strong and durable.

Chapter 22

Accounting and Bookkeeping

For must SBOs, accounting and bookkeeping are their nemeses. SBOs usually believe they can handle their own bookkeeping and rarely have a professional do it. Consequently very little bookkeeping actually takes place until an accountant is finally hired to prepare a tax return a year later. By this time the bookkeeping is of no value to the SBO as it is water under the bridge, and it may be too late to rectify the situation. To make matters worse, critical records may have been lost, which may make it impossible to create an accurate set of books.

In this day and age, when we have such accessibility to computers, there is no excuse for not keeping a good set of books. When I first started my law practice in the 70s, reconciling my bank statement was a difficult and time-consuming task that took hours. Bookkeeping had to be delegated to an accountant or bookkeeping service, as there simply wasn't time to run a business and keep accurate books. Usually by the time the bookkeeper provided financial reports, it was too late for them to be of any value in avoiding cash flow problems.

With the advent of computers, many programs were developed to assist bookkeepers with their tedious job. These programs, however, were difficult to learn and often temperamental. I remember cursing the ones I used on a regular basis and wondering if they actually saved any time. They did save time though, because they eliminated the need for doing any kind of math, which I've found many SBOs avoid at any cost.

Then there was Quicken®, and I thought God had shined down on all of us. It was so simple and made bookkeeping so easy that I quickly began pulling my financial reports every morning. If anything didn't look right, I could immediately get to the bottom of it.

So today when you can write a check and do your bookkeeping at the same time with Quicken® or Quickbooks® or one of many other bookkeeping programs, every SBO has the ability to effortlessly keep an accurate set of books and can pull up a financial report at any time. This is a tremendous tool for the SBO and solves one of his greatest problems. Yet many SBOs still don't keep books and still operate their businesses in the dark. This is just crazy.

I don't know if they are lazy, scared of new technology, or afraid to face the truth about their business. They say ignorance is bliss, but the SBO's bliss will be short lived as the fabric of the business begins to give way. It is imperative that SBO get on top of their bookkeeping. This used to be a problem; today it is easy. If you are not doing bookkeeping, stop what you're doing right now, and go buy a bookkeeping program that does your bookkeeping every time you write a check. Then spend a day or a week, if that's what it takes to learn the program, and your bookkeeping problems will be over. Don't ever write a manual check again!

Once you learn the program and know how to pull up the reports you will need from time to time, you can delegate the actual bookkeeping to someone else and get back to whatever aspect of your small business you do best. But get the program and learn how to use it properly, and you will be well on the way to making your small business prosper.

Another related issue is record keeping. Very frequently I will represent SBOs who are being audited by the IRS. If the truth were known, they would owe no taxes, but unfortunately they quite often have not kept records of their income and expenses, so when they are asked to prove the deductions they have taken they are out of luck. Every year thousands of SBOs pay hundreds of thousands of dollars in taxes they don't owe, simply because they were too lazy to get receipts, keep their invoices after they paid their bills, and keep their bank statements.

In an audit, if you can't prove your deductions, the IRS will disallow them. Conversely they will charge the SBO with income for every dollar that shows up as a deposit even if, in reality, the deposit is a redeposit or transfer of money already considered as income. If you can't prove the source of the deposit, it will be considered income and you may end up paying taxes on it twice.

Avoiding overpayment of your taxes, however, is not the only reason SBOs should keep all their records. Records are needed in litigation if you are trying to prove a claim against someone, or defending a claim asserted against you. Recently our firm has contacted all of our clients to see if they took the diet drug Fen-Phen. For those who took they drug for six months or more, it is likely they will be entitled to $500,000 in compensatory damages. All they have to do is produce doctor or prescription records showing that they used the drug for this period. Unfortunately most of those who are eligible to recover this money don't have any records to substantiate their claim. Instead, they have to hope the pharmacy or doctor has the records. Many people will not recover a dime even though they took the drug for the minimum period. This is a shame and could easily have been avoided.

Record keeping can be very time consuming and tedious work if you do a good job. But record keeping doesn't have to be all that organized to be effective. Sure, it would be best if you kept a file for every creditor, supplier, customer, and employee, and stored them neatly in a file cabinet, but that isn't absolutely necessary. The key factor is that the record must be kept. To do that all you need is a box. When a bill is paid, a bank statement reconciled or correspondence received, simply throw it in the box. When the box gets full, seal it up, date it, and get a new box. Continue to throw all your receipts, invoices, check registers, and any other written records in your storage box instead of the trash can.

Down the road if you have an audit or need to prove a claim, you can go to the storage box, dig through it, and find what you need. So from now on, don't through away any business receipts. Simply throw them in a storage box and forget about them.

Even with a good accounting program, you'll still need an accountant to do your taxes. But the cost of the accountant will be much less, because they won't have to do a year's worth of accounting before they can do the tax return. If you are reorganizing your business, it is of critical importance that you hire an accountant to do your bookkeeping and to prepare monthly financial reports to provide to the court.

With the help of an accountant, the SBO can monitor the progress in turning the businesses around. If he is not progressing, together they will figure out what further adjustments are needed to make it happen. Trying to reorganize a business without accurate financial statements is like trying to ride a bucking bronco blindfolded—a rather futile and perilous undertaking. And doing it without professional help is foolish and shortsighted.

Hiring an accountant is a little different than hiring an attorney. Most accounting firms will have the expertise to do your accounting and tax preparation. What you need to look for in an accountant is whether he is strictly a numbers man, or will he be able to give you practical advice in structuring and running your business? Will he simply be an agent for the IRS, or will he be on the lookout for ways to reduce your taxes?

Once your accountant has been selected, he needs to help you prepare a realistic budget and provide you with monthly financial reports so you can see if you are keeping within your budget goals. Sadly, few SBOs see monthly financial reports, and fewer yet ever get around to doing a budget. Yet, to successfully reorganize, these types of reports must be prepared religiously and studied carefully as soon as they come out.

Many SBO will not understand the financial statements that their accountants produce. Part of the accountant's job is to teach the SBO what the balance sheet and income statement mean. If you don't understand the reports your bookkeeper or accountant has prepared, ask questions and keep asking questions until you do understand.

If the monthly financial statements show that you are not meeting your budget goals, ask your accountant what you can do to get in line with your budget. If the problem is beyond his expertise, you may need to hire a business consultant.

Again, you have to be careful in the selection of a business consultant. Don't ever hire the one your banker or other secured creditor refers to you. He or she may be a spy for the creditor whose objective is to squeeze as much cash out of you as they can, before you go under.

Business consultants can be found at colleges and universities, in the yellow pages, on the internet, or in business journals. Try to find one with experience in your industry, if possible. The consultant's goal should be to help you with marketing and business operations that are outside the scope of your attorney's and accountant's expertise.

Business consultants often must literally go to work for the SBO for a time to really get a handle on the business and its challenges. Usually they are much less expensive than the accountant or attorney, so it is practical to have them for ten or twenty hours a week if need be. They can train the SBO in proper business practices, bookkeeping, budgeting, and marketing. They can train employees and help the SBO find customers and vendors that will help ensure   successful operations in the future.

In a recent case, an SBO died and left his business to his two sons. Fortunately, one of the sons worked in the business but, even so, his father handled most of the critical operations, so neither had the expertise to keep the business going. Although the attorney and accountant were available for consultation, the sons needed additional help. A business consultant was called in and went on-sight to help get the business under control, and then to teach the sons how to successfully run it. After six months, not only was the business still around, it was thriving and even operating more efficiently than when their father had been in charge.

Chapter 23

Changing Your Ways

Once you hire your accountant it's important to do a budget to determine what cutbacks to make. Frequently there will have to be layoffs, salary reductions, and suspensions of fringe benefits. Rent may be too high, which will require re-negotiations with the landlord, or termination of leases and executory contracts in bankruptcy.

If the SBO has been looting the company, that has to come to a halt. If the company has too many employees or simply can't afford what it has, the whole operation of the business will need to be reviewed to determine how labor can be better utilized so that fewer employees will be required.

If payroll taxes haven't been paid and proper procedures for collecting and paying these taxes aren't in place, that situation needs to be corrected immediately. It's not wise to finance your reorganization with Uncle Sam's money. It's an expensive loan, and one that will only cause you immeasurable grief in the long run.

This is a critical stage in the reorganization process and must be done as quickly as possible, for there has to be a certain amount of cash available to continue operations. If the negative cash flow isn't stopped quickly enough, the business may run out of money and be unable to reorganize at all.

Too often SBOs wait too long to seek legal counsel and the business is too far gone to be saved. It is important to be realistic and seek help at the first sign of trouble. This is another reason an ongoing relationship with an attorney is important. If the company has an attorney that it deals with on a regular basis, it is more likely the SBO will pick up the phone as soon as bad fortune rears its ugly head.

This is the time to take a good look at insurance too. Many SBOs operate without insurance. They think that insurance is a luxury that they will get down the road when they have extra money. Well, if you want to build a successful business, you have to realize a lot of things will go wrong and prepare for those eventualities. If you want to roll the dice and go naked you can, but only at your own peril.

The wise SBO will find a good insurance agent and sit down and figure out what insurance is absolutely necessary and get it in force immediately. In my experience, an SBO should have personal life insurance as well as disability, medical insurance, business interruption, automobile, general liability, workman's compensation, fire, and extended coverage on his real estate and contents insurance. Additionally, it is wise to get a blanket umbrella liability insurance policy, both personally and for your business.

This sounds like a lot, but if you shop carefully you can often get these coverages as part of a single policy, which will be much cheaper than separate policies. Personal life insurance, disability and medical coverage can often be purchased as a group policy, which is also a lot less expensive than if you purchase each individually.

A good insurance agent can handle all your insurance needs and take care of most of the onerous paperwork involved. It's a good idea to find an agent who is willing to take this burden off your shoulders and handle claims too, so that you won't be saddled with this task or have to pay an employee to handle it for you.

I have had the same insurance agent for twenty-five years and, whenever an issue comes up, I make one phone call and it is resolved. Conversely, if my agent becomes aware of industry changes or issues that I should know about, he calls me immediately. If I miss a premium, he gives me a personal phone call to remind me to pay. If you have five different insurance agents, you won't be a big enough client to warrant special attention and you won't get this kind of service.

I can't tell you how many times I have been forced to defend clients who thought they had insurance but for some reason hadn't paid the premium. Sometimes they were short on funds, but often it was as simple as forgetting to send in a change of address or the insurance notice getting lost in the mail. Defending a lawsuit can cost thousands of precious dollars that few SBOs can afford. If the lawsuit is lost, the business may be forced into bankruptcy or put out of business.

Insurance is not a luxury. It is a fundamental requirement for anyone who operates a business. Just as a policeman wouldn't go into a crack house without a bulletproof vest, neither should the SBO pass another day without adequate insurance to protect him from the perils of doing business.

Chapter 24

Funding the Turnaround

If you can avoid having to get additional financing for your business, you should do so. Loans are easy to get but hard to pay back. Unfortunately, some SBOs will have to find financing to turn around their business. Certain businesses require maintenance of large inventories, expensive equipment, or large quantities of supplies and materials that the SBO may not have the capital to purchase. This will necessitate procuring short term credit to finance these items. Unfortunately, an SBO trying to turn around a failing business is not likely to have the credit to get this type of financing.

A common source of this type of funding is the SBO's current secured lenders. Although the SBO's credit will probably be pretty bad, his creditors may be willing to loan additional funds because they don't want to have a non-performing loan. A loan default can cause them considerable problems with bank examiners, stockholders, or investors. As a result, they will often be willing to provide additional capital, provided there is sufficient collateral to cover the new advances, and prospects for a turnaround are good.

This type of financing, however, often comes with strings. The bank will be keeping a very close eye on the SBO's activities while it is funding the turnaround. It will also be expensive funding, as the bank will require a higher interest rate and a quicker payout due to the higher risks associated with the loan. You will no doubt have to personally guarantee the loan, pledge your ownership interest in the business, assign your life insurance, and bow before your loan officer whenever you see him.

If your existing lenders are not interested in advancing more funds, other possibilities include finding new investors, joint venturing projects, asset sales, and home equity loans. Of all these options, getting new investors is the best, of course, as no payback would be required.

Home equity loans are also attractive because the payback is stretched out over time. It's important, though, not to undertake a home equity loan unless you are *absolutely* sure that the turnaround will be successful. Often the equity in a SBO's home is the only asset he has. Since homesteads are, to some extent, exempt property, in most states, it would be a shame to give up this last asset and then not successfully reorganize.

Sometimes when a small business downsizes it will have assets it no longer needs. These assets can be sold to fund future operations. Another way to acquire assets needed for business operations is through joint ventures with other companies. For instance, I previously mentioned my builder client who was good at building, but couldn't handle money and had no credit. So when he wanted to start a new house, he joint ventured the project with his brother. The brother handled all the financing as his contribution to the partnership and my client built the house.

In another case of mine, an SBO was a distributor of specialized truck parts. Normally he would get orders for a part, buy the needed part, and then sell it to the customer. Unfortunately, after he filed his Chapter 13, he didn't have cash to buy the parts for resale. So what he did was get another company to buy the part, sell it to him at a little markup, and then he'd resell it to his customer. Since nobody knew who the ultimate customer was, this worked pretty well. The joint venture partner had very little risk as he usually bought on credit and was paid by my client before he had to pay the supplier.

If none of these sources of financing are available, some clients have turned to high interest lenders, some legal and some not. I have had clients who had loans with interest rates as high as 200 percent per annum. Some small lenders who make very high risk loans are allowed to charge this type of interest, but usually when you see these loan shark interest rates, the loans are not legal.

In Texas the most an unlicensed lender can charge varies from 18% to 28% percent, depending on the prime rate at the time. Other states have similar laws. Lenders get around this by setting up complicated factoring arrangements or inventory purchase agreements. Recently a client brought me one of these contracts. The way this one worked was that a lender purchased an inventory item from my client, who was a manufacturer. He then sold it at a premium to my client's customer. Theoretically, there wasn't a loan—just a purchase and sale, but actually the entire transaction was handled by the manufacturer just as if the lender wasn't involved. When I put the pencil to it, the cost to the manufacturer was the equivalent of a loan at seventy-two percent per annum.

These usurious loans should be avoided at all cost. Should you be so desperate that you need to resort to this type of lending, odds are you are not going to be successful at reorganizing. Since these loans almost always require personal guarantees and collateral assignments of your interests in the business, it is usually financial suicide to enter into them. Additionally, the people who make these kinds of loans are often shady at best, and may resort to violence should you default. So, stay clear of this type of illegal lending.

For the SBO trying to reorganize, additional debt can be very burdensome and may jeopardize his ability to successfully turn his business around. Think very carefully about whether new debt is absolutely necessary. Sure it would make things easier, but can you survive without it. If you can, then don't borrow more money. Bite the bullet and do without the new cash. In the long run, you'll be glad you did.

Chapter 25

Dealing with Depression

While you are trying to reorganize, depression will no doubt be a frequent companion. Every business owner gets depressed from time to time, but the owner who is facing a possible business failure will face an unbearable emotional strain. Worry, embarrassment, anger, frustration, fear—these emotions will become so overwhelming at times that the SBO will simply want to give up.

When I first started law practice, I got a call from a woman whose husband had committed suicide. He had a small vacuum cleaner business that hadn't been doing so well and he had become very depressed. One day his wife came home and found him dead—a self-inflicted gunshot wound to the head.

As I got into the case, I discovered that the business had some financial problems, but nothing so bad that it couldn't have been fixed. In fact, the wife's brother took over the business and we were able to successfully reorganize it under Chapter 11. As I worked on the case, I felt very sad to think that a young man took his life needlessly and for something as unimportant as money.

Other SBOs over the years have turned to drugs and alcohol as an escape from their stressful lives. This only makes matters worse and leads to other, more serious problems. In recent years I have seen two clients literally destroy their lives using illegal drugs. One committed suicide and the other one is on the brink of a mental breakdown.

Because of these sad experiences, I have made it a personal goal to help my clients avoid this type of tragedy.

Some attorneys, when they meet a client with financial troubles, are very negative and often chastise their clients for their stupidity. This is an intentional tactic designed to make the client so fearful that they will immediately do whatever the attorney asks and pay whatever he charges. This is despicable behavior and it sickens me when I see it or hear about it.

The first thing I try to do with a client is to assure him that it isn't the end of the world. Although the situation may seem bleak, the fact is there are a lots of ways to successfully reorganize a business and I am sure we will be able to come up with a viable strategy. Then I remind them that money isn't what is important in life. It is their friends and family that matter and as long as they have those things, they are blessed. I tell them to quit worrying about their creditors as I would be taking that burden off their shoulders. They usually leave very much relieved and they usually tell me so.

To successfully reorganize your business, you must be optimistic about the future. A good attorney will do his best to make you feel this way, but often that won't be enough. Things will go wrong, creditors won't always cooperate, and doubts and anxieties are bound to creep back into your mind. There are several ways to deal with fear and depression while you are trying to turn around your business. A technique that worked for me in the early years when money was tight was to work overtime.

Rather than sit at home worrying about business, I set up an office at home, and at 6:00 or 7:00 every night, I shifted my work from the office to home. By working 60 hours a week, I actually felt better because I was earning more money and directly attacking the source of my anxiety—my work. This is not the ideal solution, and it has made me a workaholic over the years, but it is better than going to a bar or to the racetrack. When money is in short supply and labor expensive, oftentimes the SBO must work long hours and wear several hats to survive.

Another technique is diversion. Over the years, spending time with my wife and children was always a great diversion. When times got particularly stressful, we'd go fishing or travel. I was always able to forget about work when I was out on the road or out at the lake. After the kids grew up, I took up writing as a diversion from my stressful law practice. This has worked well and helped me maintain my sanity during some pretty tough times.

There are hundreds of other types of diversions that can help reduce stress, such as hunting, fishing, hiking, skiing, scuba diving, hockey, basketball, football, baseball and tennis. Participating in these activities not only helps you forget about your problems, but they also keep you in better physical condition, which, in itself, helps your ability to cope with stress. Even if you don't directly participate in a sport, just being a spectator can be very beneficial by allowing you to escape into another world and forget about your troubles. SBOs should find a hobby, a sport, or other activity that they enjoy and pursue it with great enthusiasm. SBOs needs to have the ability to relax, recharge their spirit and clear their minds of worry and anxiety so that when they come to work each day, they are ready to tackle the difficult tasks that await them.

CASE STUDIES

Case Study 1

Greenbrier Cleaners

So far we've talked a lot about problems that face small business owners. I've told you some stories from my experience over the years in helping SBOs, but in order to really understand the process of defending a SBO I want to take you through an fictional example from start to finish. While the following names and events are not real, they are inspired by actual cases.

Don Parker and his wife Louise always dreamed of owning their own business. Their children were grown, and they felt it was time to make their move. They had met at TI five years earlier, after each had gone through painful divorces. They fell in love and were married. They liked their jobs, but knew their futures at TI were bleak, as the company was in one of its downsizing modes, and there was talk of layoffs. In September they were referred to an attorney by a business broker who was showing them a dry cleaning business that was for sale. When they came in to see their attorney, he went over the contract with them in detail and suggested they form a corporation to actually operate the business.

The purchase price was $180,000. The seller wanted $36,000 down and agreed to finance the balance. Of course, whenever a seller finances a portion of the sale, they retain a security interest in the business until they are paid off. This is done to guarantee that they will paid in accordance with the contact. A note was signed by Don and Louise for $144,000, amortized over five years at 10% interest.

The assets of the business consisted of equipment and leasehold furnishings with a value of $120,000, inventory of $20,000, delivery trucks worth $30,000 and cash and accounts receivable of $10,000. As part of the deal Don and Louise assumed a 4,000 square foot shopping center lease with a monthly rental of $3,600 per month. Along with these assets came a customer list with some 1,800 names, addresses, and telephone numbers.

After the corporation was set up, Don and Louise went to their local bank and set up a bank account. Then they visited their insurance agent to purchase contents coverage for the business, auto coverage for the vans as well as workmen's compensation insurance for their employees.

Being a little cash poor when they started the business, Louise had volunteered to do the bookkeeping for the business, which they decided to call Greenbrier Dry Cleaning. She didn't have any experience in bookkeeping but felt she could figure it out. Unfortunately she became so wrapped up in running the business that she was lucky to find the time to write checks to pay the bills, let alone bookkeeping or budgeting.

As part of the deal, the seller had agreed to stay on for thirty days to teach them the business. Unfortunately, Don had decided to stay on at TI for awhile until the business got going. Consequently, he missed most the training. Louise did the best she could, but it took them nearly 90 days to master the basics of operating a dry cleaning business.

During this first ninety days the business lost over $10,000, draining them of a substantial portion of their operating capital. Desperate for money to make payroll, Don borrowed $4,000 on a Visa card. With this cash they were able to survive two more weeks when, fortunately, business began to improve. They barely made payroll on the fifteenth, but managed to squeak by.

The next few months went more smoothly, but Don and

Louise still had to borrow another $3,000 on credit cards to make ends meet. By Christmas business was booming and they thought the worst was over. Then one day a letter came from their landlord advising them that their boiler had sprung a leak and was venting steam into the attic of the shopping center. Apparently this had been going on for some time, and the entire roof of the shopping center had been compromised. In the letter was a demand for $25,000 to repair the damage to the roof.

Don and Louise were devastated by the letter and didn't know what to do, so someone referred them to me. I asked them if they had insurance, and they indicated they did. I suggested they call their insurance agent and file a claim. A couple weeks later they called again and advised me that the insurance company had refused to pay the claim because the policy had a specific exclusion for the type of leak that had occurred.

As the weeks went by, the landlord grew impatient for the reimbursement for the roof repair and threatened to lock them out if they didn't pay up. By maxing out all their credit cards, getting a couple thousand dollars from family, and letting all their personal debts slide, they managed to raise fifteen thousand dollars, which bought them another month or two with the landlord.

The following week, Don got his pink slip, leaving the Parkers with no income except what the business could afford to pay them. By mid-February when they came in to see me, they were two months behind on their payroll tax deposits, owed a month and a half on the rent, hadn't paid a credit card in three months, and had $15,000 in past due accounts payables.

The first thing I made them do was a budget so we could see if the business was profitable or not. I asked the questions, they filled in the blanks. This is how it looked:

MONTHLY BUDGET PROJECTION
GREENBRIER DRY CLEANING

Income	
Sales	$30,000.00
Total Sales	$30,000.00
Expenses	
Advertising	$480.00
Automobile	$880.00
Bank Charges	$50.00
Contract Labor	$2,500.00
Insurance	$660.00
Maintenance & Repairs	$250.00
Rent	$4,800.00
Salaries	$15,000.00
Supplies	$3,010.00
Telephone	$250.00
Utilities	$1,202.00
Credit Card Min Payment	$320.00
Note Payment to Seller	$5,000.00
Total Expenses	$34,402.00
Difference	($4,402.00)

They weren't shocked to find out they were losing money, but they didn't realize how bad it was. I told them they had to get their business in the black for the business to be worth saving. If it couldn't make a profit, then they should go back to working for someone else.

The first thing I always look at is labor. Is there any way they can run the business with less help or can we find cheaper labor? They thought about this and decided, since Don was able to work full time now, that they could eliminate half of their contract labor and reduce one salaried employee for a savings of $4,200.00.

This was almost enough to get them in the black, but we needed to do better than that. We needed a surplus each month sufficient to fund a Chapter 13 or a workout with creditors. This meant we needed to know how far behind they were, so we did a spreadsheet as follows:

Creditor	Amount Due
IRS	$4,200.00
Landlord	$7,200.00
Vendors	$9,000.00
Credit Cards	$8,700.00
Total	$29,100.00

I knew in a Chapter 13 bankruptcy they could pay out any debts owed over a 60 month period. If we'd had some cash to work with, I might have suggested a workout, but that wasn't the case so the Chapter 13 was the obvious choice.

One drawback of Chapter 13 or Chapter 11 is that there are a lot of rules and guidelines that the SBO must adhere to while reorganizing. The debtor can't borrow money or sell property without first giving notice to creditors and sometimes getting a court order. The debtor must keep all his post-petition debts current, pay all taxes in a timely manner and keep his property insured. These are all good rules but sometimes difficult to follow.

Since the Parkers were retaining their business assets in Chapter 13, they were required to pay a 100% plan. Their payments turned out to be a little over $600 per month but this eliminated the $320 per month minimum payments on their credit cards. Consequently, the net increase to their monthly out of pocket cash flow was $280. This seems hard to believe, but it is made possible because there is no interest paid on unsecured debt in Chapter 13. The balance on date of filing is all that must be paid. This savings is offset somewhat by the 10% fee paid to the trustee, but still can be quite substantial.

Once the Parkers were under the protection of the court and made the necessary adjustments to their budget to become profitable, business improved dramatically. They were able to do more advertising and began contacting the people on their customer list, many of whom hadn't patronized their business in over a year. As they became more profitable they doubled up on their Chapter 13 plan payments and ended up paying the plan off in 36 months rather than 60.

Several years out of bankruptcy the Parkers were still doing well. In fact, they had expanded their operations adding another plant and two pickup stations. The same business broker who had sold them their business now was after them to put it on the market again, this time with an asking price triple what they had originally paid.

Case Study 2

Holiday Market

Back in the 1980s when there were still a lot of independent food stores around I had a client who operated half a dozen of them in the Dallas metroplex. He had acquired them from a chain store operation that had gone out of business. George Snyder was an accomplished grocer, having worked for a major chain store for over twenty years. He knew what he was doing and was often consulted by others operating retail grocery stores. In the past he had been the president of a major grocery trade organization.

At first the Holiday Markets flourished, and he was beginning to accumulate a nice estate. In fact, he first called me to do some estate planning for him. Like many SBOs, he had been so busy operating his business, he hadn't taken the time to do the basic estate planning that every SBO owner needs to do. After that project had been completed, I didn't hear from him again for over a year. Then one day George called and asked if I could come to see him.

Attorneys don't usually make house calls, but occasionally I'll have clients who expect me to come to them. I guess it's a question of whose time is more valuable. If a client thinks his time is more valuable than mine, and is willing to pay me to travel to him, I don't usually complain.

This first meeting was the first of many over the next two years as the Holiday Markets felt the squeeze from dozens of new chain supermarkets that were springing up everywhere. Fortunately, George was a fighter and was determined to stay in business. As sales slumped, he had cut overhead, increased advertising and consolidated operations between all his stores. But no matter what he did his operating capital continued to shrink until he was having severe cash flow problems.

George was a proud man, and I could tell calling me there to discuss financial problems was killing him. He and his manager were both chain smokers, and I remember the smoke was so thick that day, that I got such a terrible headache that I could hardly think. But somehow, through the smoke, I got the gist of the crisis that confronted them.

At that time supermarkets made a lot of money cashing payroll checks and selling money orders. To do this, the supermarkets contracted with a money order company that provided the blank money orders. The contract provided that all the money taken in by the supermarket was to be put in a separate trust account and remitted to the money order company at stated intervals. The store was supposed to take its cut when it remitted the money to the money order company. In practice, however, the stores would invariably put all the money order revenue into their general account and pay the money order company as a regular payable. The net effect was the store was operating on the money order company's money.

The problem that faced George and the Holiday Market was that it had an $80,000 money order payment due and no funds to pay it. It was a delicate situation, because once the money order company found out they weren't going to get paid, they would shut down the money order operations at all the Holiday locations. With no money orders available, many customers would stop cashing checks and a great deal of revenue would be lost—not only check cashing revenue, but all the sales that usually flowed from the check cashing-customers would also go by the wayside.

We discussed options, one of which was to find a substitute money order company. The problem with this was that it would take several weeks to switch companies, and the would lose a lot of business during that time period. The other obvious problem would be convincing another money order company to do business with a sinking business.

After several months of discussions and planning, we decided the only alternative was to file a Chapter 11. Charles had already reinvested all his money into the company and simply couldn't raise the funds necessary to get the business back on track. Of the six stores, only two were profitable, so the company was losing $20,000 a month. It was clear a reorganization was necessary.

After the plan was filed, the U.S. Trustee's office called us in for the initial conference. They are charged with the oversight of Chapter 11 cases, so they bring in the debtor early on to make sure they know the rules of operating in Chapter 11 and are following them. One of the first things a debtor-in-possession, as Chapter 11 debtors are called, must do is shut down the old bank accounts and open new ones. These new debtor-in-possession accounts are set up to be monitored by the U.S. Trustee's office. Monthly operating reports must be provided to the court and trustee's office so they can track the debtor-in-possession's compliance with the intricate Chapter 11 rules of operation.

Several weeks later, the trustee conducted a creditors meeting, at which time creditors and the trustee asked questions of debtor and discussed the reorganization plan. The plan that we proposed was to sell the assets of the four unprofitable stores and use that money to pay off secured debts. The unsecured creditors would be paid 25% of their debt, thus putting the company in a position that it could be profitable in the future. In Chapter 11 a debtor can affirm or reject leases. This allowed Holiday Market to get out of its leases in the four unprofitable stores so that the company could concentrate on the two profitable stores.

Although in the bigger Chapter 11 cases a creditor's

committee is usually appointed to represent all the unsecured creditors, often in smaller cases there aren't enough active unsecured creditors to have such a committee. This was the case with the Holiday Markets, and this made it easier to get our plan confirmed.

Once we propose a plan we put together a very comprehensive disclosure statement that explained the bankruptcy process to the creditors and gave them all the information about Holiday Market and its plan of reorganization such that they could vote intelligently when the plan was later put to a vote.

The plan was approved by the creditors and confirmed by the court. It was a long, expensive process, but in the end was well worth the effort. A year later one of the remaining two stores was doing very well, but the other was still struggling. George had shut down his administrative office and set up shop at the west Dallas store. The downtown Dallas store was turned over to a manager who turned out to be incompetent. Unfortunately, George didn't realize it until it was too late. Eventually that store had to be sold.

Five years later, George retired and his two sons took over the last Holiday Market. The store was highly profitable for another ten years until it was destroyed one night by a raging fire. It was never rebuilt, as the two sons feared they would never be able to get their customers back after being out of business for three or four months.

With the insurance money and proceeds of the sale of the land upon which the store had been built, the two brothers were able to open a trucking business, which they are successfully operating today.

CASE STUDY 3

TJ Handbag & Belt

Sometimes for one reason or another a client refuses to file bankruptcy even though it seems to be the way out of their financial distress. Once such case was TJ. Shah. TJ had owned a handbag and belt manufacturing plant in Euless, Texas for many years and had done very well. He owned a very expensive home as well as the land and building in which he operated his business, and had plenty of cash. Unfortunately he had only major customer, a large department store chain.

In the mid-90s his department store customer began to struggle and had to close many of its stores. As a result, the big orders for purses and belts that he had grown dependent upon dropped drastically. The retail market at the time was bad, so TJ had difficulty replacing the declining purchases from this big customer. Eventually the department store owners filed Chapter 11 and receivables in excess of $100,000 had to be written off.

When TJ came to see me he was desperate. The IRS had garnished his bank accounts, there were several lawsuits in progress, and he was getting dozens of calls each day from creditors wanting to get paid. This was an obvious situation that called for a Chapter 11, but TJ, for personal and religious reasons, wouldn't hear of it.

Prior to coming to see me, he had managed to get most of his creditors to accept payouts for what was owed them. He didn't like to pay attorneys, but needed me to defend a couple lawsuits that had been filed against him. The one that was most troublesome was from his biggest supplier who was owed $85,000. They were unsympathetic to TJ's financial situation and pressed hard for a judgement. After several months of bitter fighting, legal fees started to become a problem for TJ, and I wondered if he was going to make it. It seemed this adversary was intentionally invoking every legal maneuver in order to run up his legal bill.

TJ's biggest problem in reorganizing was getting supplies, as all his vendors had put him on a "cash only" basis. He had to have raw materials to manufacture his goods, or he wouldn't have had anything to sell. But his cash was being drained by all the installment payout arrangements he had worked out with his creditors. To preserve precious cash, he had let all but his most critical employees go and was handling sales himself. Eventually we got his lawsuits settled and his future seemed brighter. Business picked up and he was able to get a small line of credit from a new supplier. It seemed the worst was over.

TJ owed me quite a bit of money by the time I was through defending him, and I knew it would be a long time before I got paid, if at all. I didn't want to press him because of everything he had gone through already, so I just forgot about the bill. A year later out of the blue he called and said he had paid off several of the payouts and was ready to start working on my bill. I was shocked but thanked him for not forgetting about me. A day or two later he sent me 24 post-dated checks, which totaled the amount of my bill. He said just to deposit one each month.

Now TJ is back on top and business is good. His customers are more diversified now, so he shouldn't be as vulnerable to a major drop in sales. All his old creditors have been paid and he is starting to put a little money away for the next avalanche or hurricane that strikes. TJ was able to weather the storm because he owned his own building, couldn't be evicted, and he was able to cut his overhead to a bare minimum until business picked up. Most importantly, he was determined to survive and never lost heart.

CONCLUSION

No matter how desperate your situation looks, if you take a deep breath and vow to take charge of your destiny, you can do it! You have the independent spirt, the drive, and the desire to be successful. Now you know the pitfalls to avoid and the tools you will need to be successful. It's time now for performance. No more excuses or whining about how you are a victim of the economy or the competition. You have achieved the American dream of owning your own business and being truly free. Don't let it slip out of your hands.

It won't be easy. Nothing worthwhile ever is, but it will be the most fulfilling task you will ever perform. If you can turn your business around, and I know you can, you will feel an exhilaration few people have ever experienced. Your confidence will soar. Your health will improve, you will feel younger, have more energy, and you will sleep soundly at night. But the best news is that your business will begin to flourish beyond your wildest expectations, as you have learned how to run a small business.

This isn't to say you won't ever have problems again. Obviously you will, but now that you are an astute business owner, you will not be as dependent or controlled by your environment. With a lean, efficient operation you will sail through the recessions and the downturns by quickly adjusting to the marketplace. When times are good you won't loot your company but will set aside funds for future emergencies and pay off debts so that eventually you will be debt-free.

This isn't a dream or an idle fantasy. This can be your reality if you want it badly enough and are willing to make the necessary sacrifices to make it happen.

Good luck!

INDEX

GLOSSARY

Accountant - The number cruncher who all SBOs desperately need to help them keep track of their money and keep the IRS off their back.

Accounting - The boring, tedious process of keeping track of your money so you know if you are making or losing it.

Attachment - a legal method available to judgment creditors allowing them to seize assets belonging to a judgment debtor.

Attorney - The greedy but streetwise SOB every business owner desperately needs in order to survive and thrive as a SBO.

Automatic stay - a federal court order that takes effect immediately upon filing on a bankruptcy and stops creditors from taking any further action to collect the debts owed them by the debtor.

Board of directors - the group of men elected by the shareholders who are charged with the responsibility of operating the corporation between annual shareholder meetings. They typically elect officers to run the business on a day-to-day basis but make the important decisions.

Budget - An estimate of future income and expenses of the business over a period of time.

Cash flow - The total amount of cash received by an SBO, from whatever source, less all expenditures for a given period.

CFO (Chief Financial Officer) - the person responsible for the financial well being of a business.

Collateral - property of the business that is pledged as security for the payment of a debt.

Competition - Other businesses in your neighborhood that provide goods or services similar to yours.

Confirmation - the process of approving a Chapter 11 or Chapter 13 reorganization plan.

Contract labor - Persons who work for more than one employer, part time or as needed, and are not under the direct control of the SBO.

Constable - A law enforcement officer of a local government who often serves legal papers or tries to collect or enforce judgments of the civil courts.

Creditor's meeting - A meeting required in all bankruptcy proceedings, at which time the trustee and creditors can ask questions of the debtor. It is sometimes called a 341 meeting named after the bankruptcy code section from which it is authorized.

Debtor - A person or business entity that owes money to someone else; a person who has filed bankruptcy.

Debtor Adjustment - A Chapter 13 bankruptcy.

Debtor-in-possession - A person or business entity that has filed a chapter 11 bankruptcy and remains in control of their business while it is reorganized.

Defensive estate plan - The structure of a person's financial affairs such that it is not vulnerable to sudden attack and loss to predators.

Disclosure Statement - a document required in a chapter 11 case that provides the creditors with full disclosure of the chapter 11 process, the history of the debtors, and the terms of the proposed chapter 11 plan of reorganization.

Execution - The legal process by which a sheriff or constable attempts to collect a judgment from the judgment debtor.

Embezzlement - When a trusted employee or family member steals money from you a little at a time so it goes unnoticed.

Exempt property - The property, as provided by federal or state laws, which a debtor in bankruptcy can keep and won't lose after filing bankruptcy. Also, that property by state law that is protected from execution by judgment creditors.

Garnishment - A collection method available to judgment creditors that compels third parties to pay over money they owe to the judgement debtor to them instead.

General Partnership - A type of business relationship where individuals act together in a business venture sharing profits, losses and liabilities. It is generally not a preferred way to do business and should be avoided.

Joint Venture - Another term for a general partnership which is usually not a preferred way to do business.

Judgment Creditor - A creditor who has obtained a judgment from a court of law fixing the amount owed to him by a debtor.

Judgment Debtor - A person or business entity that has a

judgment rendered against them by a court of law, fixing the amount that is owed.

Loan consolidation - The process of paying off several small loans from the proceeds of a bigger loan, hopefully at a lower interest rate, payable over a longer term and with lower monthly payments.

Looting - The common practice of small business owners to suck every dollar they possibly can from their businesses to support their lavish lifestyles until the business can't support itself and goes under.

Member - One of the owners of a limited liability company, called an LLC, (like a shareholder of a corporation). The members usually run the LLC without of board of directors.

Non-recourse debt - A form of secured debt that, in the event of a default, the creditor will take the collateral in full satisfaction of the debt and not seek damages from the business or its owners.

Partners - The owners of a partnership whether it be a general partnership, limited partnership or joint venture.

Plan of Reorganization - The plan a debtor-in-possession files in a Chapter 11 bankruptcy proceeding.

Plan payment - The amount of money a debtor must pay each month to creditors in a chapter 11 or chapter 13 bankruptcy.

Plastic - Credit cards

Post-Petition - The period of time after a bankruptcy is filed.

Predators - Greedy individuals and business entities that search out of ways take money away from honest, hard-working SBOs, and sometimes called "vultures."

Pre-petition - The period of time before a bankruptcy is filed.

Pro se defendant - A defendant who answers a lawsuit himself without obtaining legal counsel—otherwise known as an "idiot."

SBO - Small business owner

Standing Chapter 13 Trustee - The trustee who oversees and administers all chapter cases in a particular district.

Stockholders/shareholders - the owners of a corporation

Suffocation - The tendency of small businesses owners to have too much overhead, the cost of which will eventually put them out of business

Trustee - A person who is appointed by the U.S. Trustee's office to oversee a bankruptcy proceeding; a person who is appointed to handle a fund of money under a trust instrument

United States Trustee - the person who oversees all bankruptcies that are filed in a particular district.

MARY KLAASEN, Ph.D.

Since 1979, Dr. Klaasen has consulted with many start-up businesses in their strategic and system planning, exccutive, financial, and markcting developmenl, and relationships of corporate owners with stockholders and boards.

In addition to consulting, she spent 10 years as an owner and manager of a retail business, one year selling for a major British retailer, and three years as national marketing and advertising director for a chain of 70 bookstores.

Dr. Klaasen has a Ph.D. in management with specialties in organization structures, systems, and corporate culture. Clients include businesses in restaurant and food service, retail, and service sector enterprises. Mary's focus is on business results and systems with an emphasis on value and efficiency.

Fiction by William Manchee

Twice Tempted

Undaunted

Brash Endeavor

Death Pact

Second Chair

Trouble In Trinidad

Cash Call

Plastic Gods

For more information on William Manchee visit:

http://williammanchee.com

http://toppub.com

or call 972-490-9686